THE
BED BUG
BOOK

The
BED BUG

The Complete Guide to
Prevention and
Extermination

Book

RALPH H. MAESTRE

Board-Certified Entomologist

Skyhorse Publishing

I would like to thank my editor, Jennifer McCartney, for taking a chance on me and assisting me every step of the way.

Skyhorse Publishing books may be purchased in bulk at special discounts for sales promotion, corporate gifts, fund-raising, or educational purposes. Special editions can also be created to specifications. For details, contact the Special Sales Department, Skyhorse Publishing, 307 West 36th Street, 11th Floor, New York, NY 10018 or info@skyhorsepublishing.com.

Skyhorse® and Skyhorse Publishing® are registered trademarks of Skyhorse Publishing, Inc.®, a Delaware corporation.

www.skyhorsepublishing.com

10 9 8 7 6 5 4 3 2 1

Library of Congress Cataloging-in-Publication Data available on file
ISBN: 978-1-61608-299-4

Printed in the United States of America

To my loving wife Paula
and my children Jonathan and Faith.

CONTENTS

• CHAPTER 4 •

Guide to Treatments   69

• CHAPTER 5 •

Case Studies   103

* CHAPTER 6 *

What the Near and Distant Future Holds 133

* CHAPTER 7 *

104 Things to Know About Bed Bugs 141

Final Thoughts 167

Appendix A 169

Appendix B 173

References 179

ACKNOWLEDGMENTS

There are individuals in life who become mentors because they wish to pass on their knowledge with the passion they developed for the subject matter in their own lives. Those who influenced me placed me on a path I didn't foresee when I was deciding about my career. I had developed a love for biology in high school. Entering college, I thought I would go on to medical school. That was not the case. For ten years I did a little of this and a little of that. I lost my way during that time.

In the fall of 1992, I returned to college attending City University of New York at Queens College. This is where I met my first mentor, Dr. Milton Nathanson, the guidance counselor who placed me in the sequence of comparative, field, and environmental biology. To fulfill some required courses I had to take invertebrate zoology, entomology, and parasitology as an undergraduate with Dr. David Alsop. Dr. Alsop is a special individual who showed a passion for the subject matter unlike anyone else I met. I would go on to take entomology and parasitology at the graduate level with him as well. What Dr. Alsop taught me in zoology Dr. Jon Sperling taught me in botany. These men were exceptional in field. Few universities within the New York City area have this strength. I still keep in contact with Dr. Alsop.

During this entire time, I worked full-time in the pest management industry and was courting my wife. Having lost my father as a teenager, I now lost my mother to cancer in 1999. This turned my life upside down. I would end the development of my own pest management company and sell it to the company I currently work with, Magic Pest Management.

I changed my major from biology to environmental science due to my responsibilities at my new job. I had already met most of the course requirements. This would allow me to complete my degree in a shorter time. I had been taking courses from 1992 through 2007. All of this was done in the evening.

In the environmental science department I met Dr. George Hendrey, who gave me the encouragement to complete my final course in 2007. He accepted a research paper on termites that I put my heart and soul into.

During this same time, I studied and passed my board certification exams with the Entomological Society of America in General entomology and Urban and Industrial entomology. I have been a member of the society since 1997.

Within the industry of pest management are several individuals that have become my mentors. The first is the mentor to many others, Dr. Austin Frishman. My only regret is not having met him earlier when he taught in Farmingdale. He is by far the greatest influence in our industry. I work with Lynn Frank, the technical director of Suburban Pest Management located in Smithtown, New York, and a former student of Dr. Frishman. Another former student I have the pleasure of knowing is Dr. Robert Corrigan, the ultimate rodentologist. Dr. Corrigan, known as Bobby, is now a consultant for the New York City Department of Health and Mental Hygiene's Rodent Division.

I work with a great team of individuals who I wish to acknowledge. Darin Byer, the next generation at Magic; Anthony DeVito, ACE, the general manager at Magic; James Tallman and Michael Morales, ACE, our service managers who, on a day-to-day basis, solve pest problems. The opportunity that Hal Byer, the owner of Magic, has given me. This I appreciate beyond his knowing. Thank you, Hal.

I would like to extend a special thanks to the National Pest Management Association for their efforts in bringing this industry into a profession. Extending this same thanks to the two main trade magazines which deliver vital up-to-date information on a monthly basis: *Pest Management Profession* and *Pest Control Technology*.

Finally there is my family. My big brother, Aramis, who is nineteen years older than me yet has influenced me more than he realizes. Then there is my loving wife, Paula, who is patient with me beyond belief. I do love you. My beloved children, Jonathan and Faith, they are the reason for everything I do. I hope to leave a better planet for them to enjoy.

INTRODUCTION

I started this project with the intention of creating a book about bed bugs that everyone would understand. I want it to intrigue, horrify, entertain, and be useful. Bed bugs infestations seem to be everywhere—the radio, television, newspapers, and the Internet. All kinds of stories and speculations have been spread. Questions have arisen that must be answered. Where to start has been the hardest part. I have been in the pest management industry for over twenty-five years now. I have an environmental science degree and I am board certified as an urban entomologist with the Entomological Society of America. I have been a member of the Society since 1997 when I was a student at Queens College, New York. I currently work as the technical director at Magic Pest Management LLC in the Greater New York area.

I have experienced different paranoid episodes concerning insects during this time. But nothing like I've ever experienced matches the paranoia that bed bugs cause. It is something about them, their nocturnal, transient, and elusive behavior that inspires fear, disgust, and indignation. Bed bugs are immediately associated with the idea of poverty, dirt, and clutter. A kind of plague. This stereotype is not true and unjust. Anyone and everyone may get bed bugs sooner or later. No one wants to be infested or thought of as being the instrument that causes the infestation. Little experience and little knowledge of how to combat these minute vampires—because that is what they are—existed at the turn of the twenty-first century. The books were old and the pest management industry had other concerns with battling ants, stinging insects, cockroaches, flies, mosquitoes, and other pests. All that has changed because of the sudden rise in bed bug reports and infestations—the bed bug is rapidly becoming the most common pest that the pest management industry has to deal with.

Early in my line of business, the cockroaches were everywhere. The industry rotated different families of chemicals to suppress the ability of cockroaches to reproduce at alarming rates. Within a three-month period, cockroaches are capable of producing over four hundred offspring. The roach baits became the magic bullet in the early nineties.

Fleas are another pest that have always been seasonal. Then came the insect growth regulators and everything changed for the better. Insect growth regulators are synthetic hormones that prevent the juvenile insect from maturing and sterilizes the adults. I have seen the long-horned

Asian beetle which threatens entire forests. The Argentine ants that can overwhelm homes with their numbers. The marmorated brown stink bug which likes to overwinter indoors and can damage the grapevines that provide us with wine. The odorous house ants and others will still likely have their moment in the sun. Some of these problems are still emerging today. This leads to more questions that need to be answered.

Our reliance on chemicals to solve our pest problems has shown a weakness in our approach to pest management. The idea of *not* harming our properties, children, companion animals, and ourselves should be paramount. Since the first half of the twentieth century, we learned to use an agricultural technique known as integrated pest management (IPM). This approach is to utilize a combination of inspection and education, creating a plan of action that may include exclusion, sanitation, environmental modifications, behavioral changes, and finally chemical application. This approach has always been difficult for the average person to fully understand because the urge to chemically bomb our apartments can be tempting when faced with an infestation. Today, this integrated approach to pest control is known as the green approach. As for the use of pesticides, they have *always* been a tool for short-term solutions. It can't solve the problem forever.

Since we all live on the planet together, it is very important that the materials we use for controlling pests don't cause other environmental problems. We need to be vigilant—in both the production of the pesticide products and the way the Pest Management Professionals use it.

We have no intentions, as professionals, in harming what we call nontarget species. It is this intertwined relationship with all other species on Mother Earth that we fail to remember. The web of life is affected by what we do. Dinosaurs were on this earth for a very long time. They may have survived as birds, but their dominance on earth is done. Does it matter to us whether or not our species survives? I think so. I want to leave this earth to my children better than how my parents left it for me. I want future generations to enjoy the diversity of animals on this planet and not just read about it. This holds true for the vast majority of colleagues I work with in the pest management field. They wish to make a living by freeing all of us of the many pests that destroy our homes and crops. The industry helps control the many pests that harm our children, companion animals, livestock, and us. We wish to do this without causing harm while using the products we use.

Bed bugs present a difficult dilemma in that for the first time in a long time, we will use more products *in combination and quantity* while treating for bed bugs than for any other pest in a long time. This multi-product process presents challenges that we as an industry are doing our best to learn from.

In this book we will tackle only bed bugs. In doing so, we will need to overlap into other areas of pest control or management to see what will work and what will not.

I will start by giving a history lesson that I hope to make interesting. Following the history, I will deal with the life cycle of the bed bug, the way it bites, and its place in the web of life. I've included a guide to good treatment practices and will include many of today's IPM techniques. Once the foundation and understanding of these small creatures is established, then I will give case studies based on real-life circumstances that readers may relate to.

The effect that bed bugs have on the human psyche—the psychology surrounding bed bug paranoia—is interesting in itself. I do not profess to be an expert in this area—just a participant. Sometimes my associates or I intensify the client's anxiety simply by being present. I am still learning more every day about the insect world and how complex it really is. Bed bugs are no exception to this rule. It may seem simple to just get rid of them. But as many of us can testify, it costs hundreds of dollars and months of mental anguish before life returns to normal. I hope *The Bed Bug Book* helps to ease the process for those going through it as well as the individuals that are *about* to go through it. This rise of the bed bugs is going to get a lot worse before it gets better. For the bed bug is the true vampire on this earth and that really, really, sucks.

R. H. Maestre, 2011

THE
BED BUG
BOOK

CHAPTER 1

HISTORY OF
BED BUGS

For centuries, the common bed bug, *Cimex lectularius*, was the most hated of household pests. In England as late as the 1930s, over half the eight million residents were reported to have bed bugs. Infestations were rampant, extermination was difficult, and treatments were sometimes as risky to people as to pests. In battling today's global resurgence of bed bugs, much can be learned from the past. If history repeats itself, the bed bug could again become the stuff of nightmares as stated by Dr. Potter's article in *Pest Management Magazine*. We must learn quickly from our mistakes in the past and quickly find a solution. I do not want to wait until 50 percent of the residents in New York City have bed bugs to come up with a solution.

When *Homo sapiens* first emerged on this earth thousands of years ago, thousands of species of plants and animals were already established. Insects of all kinds flourished in the prehistoric climate, and today insects still outnumber all other animals on this planet. One order of insects coleoptera, the beetles, outnumbers all other animal species combined, except the microscopic organisms. They have over three hundred thousand species and counting. I have clients describe beetles over the telephone and ask me to identify them. "It's a small beetle that is black and oval—now what is it?" My answer is almost always the same, "Well, we've narrowed it down to only 300,000 species." I always ask them to mail it in for a proper identification or take a picture and e-mail it to me. Of course the truth is I can make an educated guess by narrowing it down to time of year the beetle was found and the area where the insect was discovered. This process is inaccurate, but it will narrow it down to only a few. The client may help by taking a picture and e-mailing it to their county cooperative extension office or university entomology department. I am willing to receive samples or pictures for identification purposes.

Even during the prehistoric period, around the end of the last ice age ten thousand years ago, the human species was not free from torment by insects. We were afflicted with lice and probably fleas. Nit picking was not only a social activity that emotionally bound us but it also brought relief to a degree. Nits, the eggs of lice attached to our hairs, were also a small source of protein. I know it sounds disgusting to picture this today, but it was reality then.

The males hunted small game and, in a cooperative effort, would occasionally bring down larger game such as buffalo, deer, antelope, or even an elephant. Every part of the animal was used, including the meat, fur, and bones; the meat for food, the fur for clothing and bedding, and the bones for food and tools. With the animal dead, the parasites on the fur would jump to the clan members. In some cases, the parasite would spread disease and kill them.

Soon in areas near mountains, the nomadic groups found caves and explored them. They found the shelter the caves offered would protect the clan from the cold, heat, wind, and rain. With the conquest of fire, they explored deeper into the shelter, wary of "monsters" in the form of wild animals.

With the cave to call home came the setting up and interior decorating. They didn't hang curtains, but they may have hung furs near the opening to prevent cold winds from entering. Inside, though, not all of the monsters were removed. Although the fires kept many of predators at bay, some smaller ones still roamed inside. Bats were common. They would fly out every night to return the next morning.

It is at this point that our little vampires and the myths surrounding them begin. "The Russian investigator Vlasov (1929) found a species of bed bugs on the excreta of bats in the vaults of a cave. It is from this he formulated the hypotheses that bed bugs commenced to parasitize mankind when he began to dwell in caves." (Mallis 1964)

Imagine you are in the cave with the rest of the clan while the bats begin their nightly exodus from the cave. You are afraid that they may attack, bite, or get tangled in your hair. You duck and hide. This goes on anywhere from a few minutes to close to an hour. This repeats in the morning when they return.

Something else happens during this time. When you awake the next morning, you find that you have been bitten on the exposed areas of your body. Some members of the clan think that when the bats fly in and out, that they may be biting clan members. Is this the start of the vampire bat stories? Soon it is discovered that within the cave are small insects that crawl down from where the bats roost and bite clan members. As time goes on in the cave, these same insects no longer go back to the bats but stay inside the folds of the fur blankets. The clan members at first throw out the infested furs and now have to go out and kill additional animals for new furs. Thus the first bed bugs began their torment.

Classical Period before the Roman Empire

Soon in areas like the Middle East along the Fertile Crescent, between the Tigris and Euphrates Rivers, we discovered how to plant and harvest the crops. The first homes are built along the riverbanks in order to facilitate irrigation. Small city-states are formed. Clans form large family groups and settle along the riverbanks. When they come down from the hills, they bring their blankets and clothing from the caves. With them come the bed bugs. In close quarters, with homes sharing common walls to save time and labor, bed bugs traverse the small cracks and openings, and the infestations become widespread.

How did these individuals combat the onslaught of the first bed bug infestations within the first cities? Some help came from throwing out the infested items. But again the mistake of dragging the items to the fires or outside the city walls only spread the problem. The wealthy would have slaves and servants replace bedding and clean the homes every day. This would in turn reduce the overall number of bed bugs and keep infestations suppressed. So the key elements for control during this period were sanitation and exclusion. I mention this because these are the first steps in an IPM program. "Chemical" treatments at this time may have included a cup or saucer full of oil under each foot of the bed to prevent the bugs from climbing up. Bed designs began to change from the mattress of straw on the floor to some sort of elevated platform with legs. Again, the poor who could not afford these luxuries suffered the most.

Found bed bugs were squashed by hand. Women would use small sticks or feathers to remove the ones hiding in the cracks and crevices along the wall and the joints of the furniture. These techniques were handed down from mother to daughter for generations. However, like many other hardships suffered during this time, the prevailing attitude of the population was that bed bugs were sent by the gods to punish people for not following the rules.

As cities grew, job specialization took place. New government positions were created, city planners being one of them. These individuals answered directly to the king or magistrate of the town, village, or city. Their jobs were to create roads, issue building permits, and create zoning regulations. The city planners would survey the land and establish access to clean water, etc. Managing garbage and

preventing outbreaks of disease fell under their job responsibilities. How would they have handled an outbreak of
bed bugs? No one knows for sure. Most likely everyone
tolerated a certain level of infestation in any given home.
Individuals would remove the bed bugs found by hand and
apply ineffective oils or poultices into cracks and crevices
where the bed bugs hid. The government's first document-
ed concern about bed bugs is often the same concern as
today: tourism—specifically, places of accommodations for
travelers. No village, town, or city wanted to have the repu-
tation of being infested with bed bugs or anything else. The
tavern had to maintain some sort of level of respectability.

**The Greeks were well acquainted with these
pests. In one of Aristophanes' plays, *The Clouds*,
he writes the following:**
  Socrates: Here Strepsiades, bring me a bed.
  **Strepsiades: But I can't. The bed bugs won't let
me.**

Roman Empire Period

The Roman period brought luxuries. Indoor plumbing, indoor bathrooms, beds, chairs, furniture, and other items
were designed and used throughout the Empire.

Goods arrived from all over the known world. This
would be especially true in the large cities such as Rome.

The bed bugs were transported in ships where the dark cracks and crevices would provide these little vampires with the means to populate in great numbers. Bed bugs would hide in the fabrics so the ships certainly arrived to their destination with the "finer things" in life.

The Romans named the bed bugs "*Cimex,*" which would become their genus name. The Romans found these creatures in great abundance and were at a loss as to what to do with them—until they commenced to consume the bugs in liquid concoctions as an antidote for snakebites and other assorted maladies. Bed bugs were thought to have medicinal purposes up until the nineteenth century, when they were recommended for treating hysteria.

The Romans subsequently developed pest control methods and these ideas were spread throughout the empire. In 200 BC, Roman Censor Cato encouraged the use of oils as a means of pest control and in AD 70 Pliny the Elder wrote that galbanum resin (from the fennel plant) should be added to sulfur in order to discourage mosquitoes. In 13 BC the first recorded rat-proof grain store was built by the Romans. From the year 300 BC, there is evidence of the use of predatory insects to control pests, although this method was almost certainly developed before this date.

The Romans were very resourceful, learning from other individuals as the empire grew. We all lost something when the empire collapsed. For many centuries, much of the pest management knowledge was lost.

Middle Ages through the Nineteenth Century

We take sleeping in a bedroom for granted now, but in the Middle Ages a separate room for sleeping was a luxury that only the wealthiest could afford. Cottagers slept on stone slabs covered with a thin mattress of hay or peat moss. Their one-room cottages were kept warm by an open fire in the middle of the room. In the winter, when all the windows were shuttered, the air was thick with smoke. Dew collected on the thatched roof would drip from the rafters in the morning, and when it rained no one could sleep. Small birds, mice, and insects living in the roof would scatter debris down on those sleeping below. And if that wasn't enough, the wind would whistle and moan through the chinks in the walls all night long.

A wealthy landowner or town merchant could afford better accommodations for sleeping. A bed with a mattress, sheets, blankets, canopy, curtains, etc, was the most expensive piece of furniture in most homes, and they were often mentioned in wills. The beds were often very large, and the whole family could sleep together. Guests were sometimes offered a spot in the communal bed by the fire. It was not uncommon to visit with your friends while sitting fully clothed in bed.

Queen Elizabeth had a large bed, but her ladies-in-waiting slept on straw pallets on the floor of her chamber. Many of these ladies had fine beds in their own homes with feather beds (a kind of down-filled coverlet) laid over

Detail from *Poverty* by Jean Fouquet showing
a poor person's bed with chamber pot underneath.
The bed is basically a crib filled with loose hay.

heavy canvas-covered mattresses filled with wool, straw, or moss. Henry VIII had a straw mattress that was changed every day; however, most mattresses were only changed once a year.

Lice, fleas, and bed bugs made themselves at home in beds and were a part of life. Tightly woven mattress covers called ticking helped to prevent the spread of insects—as did keeping bedding in cedar chests. But other customs like using fur coverlets and feather pillows attracted pests. Even the king's chamber was plagued with these tiny guests.

> In medieval times it was "thought to be manly to have fleas and lice and not to discourage them. St. Francis of Assisi used to refer to body parasites as 'pearls of poverty,' and the more parasites you had the holier you were."(Fagerlund 2003)

During the middle ages, insects were free for study and speculation because they were generally regarded as having originated spontaneously from air, dew, filth, and by other inconsequential means and were therefore not created by God. Accordingly, they were not given the same regard and protection as many other animals that came under the supervision of the church. As a matter of fact, the church frequently pronounced maledictions against certain groups of insects and even excommunicated them. The law also went to the extent of prosecuting them for the destruction of property, banishing them from their places of habitation, and in decreeing capital punishment for them. (Weiss 1926, 1937)

One misconception about bed bugs which has been propagated online is that the bed bug was the cause of the black plague. Bed bugs did not cause the bubonic plague. Fleas did. The black plague came from:

[T]welve trading ships from central Asia. They docked in Italy. The crew was either dead or dying. They were sent away, but it was too late. The plague began to spread. The bubonic plague was caused when a flea infected with the bacteria, *Yersinia pestis,* bit a human. The flea's bite sent the bacteria into a person's lymphatic system. Painful bumps, called buboes, developed in the groin, armpits, or neck. If the bumps broke open and the poisonous bacteria spilled out, a person could survive the disease. If the bumps did not break open, people died less than three days later. (Elliot 2006)

That fact that various sites on the Internet talk about the bed bug as the cause of the plague demonstrates how careful you should be about information you find online—misinformation can be costly, especially when dealing with bed bugs.

The term "Cimices" was used in designating bed bugs up until the seventeenth century (a plural form of the Roman *Cimex*) until the English "bed bug" became more common. "Bug" is thought to derive from the old English word "bogy," or "hobgoblin," and means "a terror in the dark." A most appropriate name for the "bogy" that invades our beds. This six-legged vampire has also been referred to as the "mahogany flat," "red coat," "wall louse," or "chinch" (Mallis 1964).

With the colonist came the bed bugs to the North American continent. It appears that the Native Americans didn't have a word for bed bugs. It is scientist and explorer Pehr Kalm who wrote in 1748 that the bed bugs were plentiful in the English colonies and in Canada but unknown amongst the Native Americans (since these little vampires inspire such fear and loathing in everyone they affect, the lack of a proper Native American name or mythology suggests this was the case).

The colonists brought them in the traditional way, by ship. They spread in this country along the trade routes. The bed bug was then transported by horse and carriage, then when the steam train was invented, by rail. The inns along the road or nearest the train stations had the worst reputations.

At the age of seventeen, our first president, George Washington, surveyed almost the entire Shenandoah Valley in the colony of Virginia. On his first trip, he was invited to stay in a frontiersman's cabin and given the only bed in the place. Before very long, he found out he wasn't alone in the bed. It was filled with bed bugs. He decided to spend the night with the other members of the party in the big room by the fire (Shaughnessy 2009).

Nineteenth Century

Old sailing ships were notoriously infested with bed bugs— some ships forbade passengers and colonists from bringing bedding on board. With the tremendous growth of the British Empire, India, Africa, South America, and Asia, bed bugs were spread around the world. The biggest difference I see between then and now is the sanitation practices in the major cities. London, England, must have been a stinky place. Sewage was commonly thrown onto the city streets where gutters allowed the flow to take the sewage into the neighboring rivers. By the end of the century, construction of sewer tunnels underground help with the sewerage transportation above ground. My understanding is that it deposited this same sewage just outside of town and the

In 1726, a gentleman by the name of John Southall, a businessman from London, visited the island of Jamaica where he encountered an elderly Jamaican man. This Jamaican was in his nineties and in very good health when Southall met him. The former slave, now a local folk doctor, noticed that Southall was scratching himself and recognized "chintzes" as the cause of his discomfort. The doctor prescribed a special remedy that he had formulated. Southall tried the concoction and to his surprise, it worked. Southall wanted to take this product back to London, England, so he got the good doctor drunk and convinced him reveal the formula. He took the formula back to England and began to sell it. Now Mr. Southall was in the pest control business. In 1730, Mr. Southall wrote a small book on his studies of the bed bug called, *A Treatise of Buggs*. He suggested,

> Persons about taking houses, lodgings, or buying furniture . . . shall be attended, and at first view be justly and truly informed if the premises be buggy, or free from Buggs.

He and his secret formula remained successful until his death (Mallis 1997).

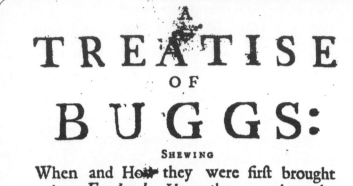

A
OF
TREATISE
BUGGS:

SHEWING

When and How they were firſt brought into *England*. How they are brought into and infect Houſes.

Their Nature, ſeveral Foods, Times and Manner of Spawning and Propagating in this Climate.

Their great INCREASE accounted for, by Proof of the Numbers each Pair produce in a Seaſon.

REASONS given why all Attempts hitherto made for their Deſtruction have proved ineffectual.

VULGAR ERRORS concerning them refuted.

That from *September* to *March* is the beſt Seaſon for their total Deſtruction, demonſtrated by Reaſon, and proved by Facts.

Concluding with

DIRECTIONS for ſuch as have them not already, how to avoid them; and for thoſe that have them, how to deſtroy them.

By *JOHN SOUTHALL*,

Maker of the Nonpareil Liquor for deſtroying *Buggs* and *Nits*, living at the *Green Poſts* in the *Green Walk* near *Faulcon-ſtairs, Southwark*.

LONDON: Printed for J. ROBERTS, near the *Oxford-Arms* in *Warwick-Lane*. M.DCC.XXX.

(Price One Shilling.)

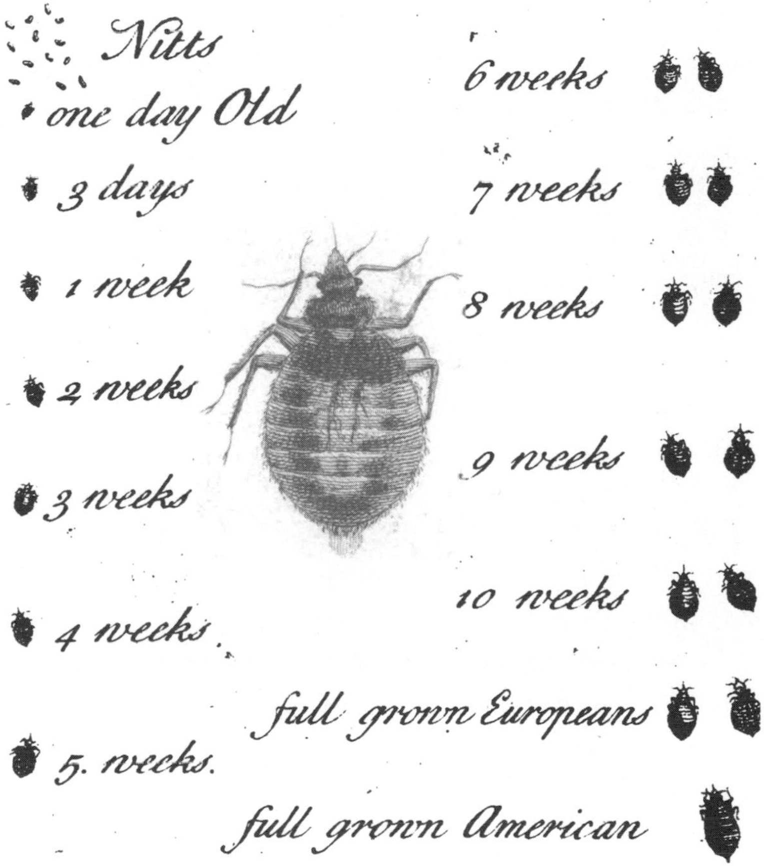

Nitts

one day Old

3 days

1 week

2 weeks

3 weeks

4 weeks

5. weeks.

6 weeks

7 weeks

8 weeks

9 weeks

10 weeks

full grown Europeans

full grown American

stench still drifted toward the city. Again, the tolerance of the population amazes me. The populous still believed that bed bugs we part of everyday life. As the population grew within the city, so did the bed bugs.

City living conditions in North America usually meant overcrowded tenement houses sharing a common bathroom down the hall or outside. Small fireplaces would have been the only source of heat for families and the bed bugs. The bed bugs would be a seasonal pest during this time. With decreased temperatures, the breeding process would slow down—bed bugs are cold-blooded creatures that cannot regulate their own body temperature like humans can. (Bed bugs are no longer seasonal pests because most homes now have central heating, which enables the bed bugs to breed consistently year-round.) At spring cleaning, the family furniture would receive a dose of boiling water to kill the bed bugs living inside. Women may have employed oil, kerosene, or other liquids to combat an infestation.

By the end of the century, pyrethrum dust became available for treating bed bugs. "Dust between the sheets of a bed, it will protect the sleeper from the most voracious bug." (USDA Division of entomology bulletin 1896).

Early Twentieth Century

By the beginning of this century, we see that bed bugs were going for a ride.

UNION PACIFIC SENDS OUT TRAIN TO EXTERMINATE VERMIN

An extra train, called the "Bed bug Special," has just been sent out by the Union Pacific to exterminate bed bugs and other vermin in the section houses along the road. It is equipped with steam hose, poisons and disinfectants. Steam from the engine will be used.

New York Tribune, September 4, 1905

THE "BED BUG" SPECIAL

Probably the only train in the world of its kind and name is now going over the main line and branches of the Union Pacific. It is equipped with all modern appliances for exterminating bugs and insects of all kinds, and will fumigate all the section houses on the system. Steam from the engine is carried to the car where it is mixed with poisons or disinfectants according to requirements, and the building sprayed inside and out by means of hose and suitable nozzles.

Popular Mechanics, November 1905

WWII through the 1990s

Bed bugs were a consistent problem on US bases during WWII. Soon after the war the availability of DDT, a chlorinated hydrocarbon (which is now known to linger for up to ten years in the environment) was used in a concentration of 5 percent as an effective spray that was applied to all household items. Initially, it demonstrated successful bed bug control for several years. But as early as 1948, two scientists named Johnson and Hill found bed bugs to be DDT resistant both in the field and laboratory. They observed several instances where DDT deposits failed to control the bed bugs in barracks of the naval receiving station in Pearl Harbor (Mallis 1997).

When DDT is applied to a surface the water carrier evaporates, leaving behind a layer of crystals. These crystals attach themselves to the body of the insects including

PHOTO BY: *Pinto and Associates*

One of the first mass-produced bed bug treatments. The level of DDT in the dust version was typically 10 percent.

the bed bug, are absorbed into its circulatory system, then reach the nervous system. When it hits the nervous system, it kills the insect.

In 1972, DDT was banned for use in the United States. This was due to the fact that the material had a long residual property that accumulated as it moved through the food chain. Rachael Carson made note of this in her book, *Silent Spring*. It was found that as mosquitoes treated with DDT died, small birds would eat the mosquitoes, and DDT would accumulate inside the birds' bodies. When a larger bird of prey ate the small birds, the DDT would be passed on. Those birds would suffer from the side effects when the eggs they laid would not hatch—DDT caused a thinning of the egg shells.

The National Pest Control Association in 1956 recommended the use of 2 percent malathion spray against the DDT-resistant bed bugs. Malathion is a very stinky material. Most people must have objected to the odor. On the other hand, many of the older Pest Management Professionals who have been around for more than twenty years remember individuals screaming at us if the product didn't smell strongly enough!

The Last Two Decades

In the early 1990s, organophosphates or carbamates were the most common products used against bed bugs. These chemicals provide a residual that allowed them to last anywhere from two to nine weeks—killing bed bugs long after the actual treatment was administered. Both organophosphates and carbamate were reasonably priced and easy to mix with water or oil. This would also allow the chemicals to be applied quickly and efficiently. They were also moderately toxic to humans, and because of this they were no longer in use by the end of the decade. Luckily, bed bug calls were few. Our concerns about the diminishing choices for treating bed bugs were also few. The industry began to use an IPM or integrated pest management program to control many pests. *Integrated pest management makes use of a combination of two or more of the following: inspection, biological, physical or environmental alterations, and chemical methods to control a pest problem.* The baits or gels used to control cockroaches and ants were successful and allowed our industry to reduce the overall amount of pesticides used in and around homes. We learned more about the behaviors of specific pests and attacked the different life cycle stages with different products. Bed bugs were not an issue. I personally encountered bed bugs two or three times between 1990 and 1999.

What was happening during this quiet period, however, was setting the stage for today's rampant infestations. All of us were traveling more and to more exotic places—much like our seafaring ancestors. Eastern Europe, Asia, Africa, Central America, and South America became far more affordable and accessible. This allowed pockets of bed bugs to hitch a ride back home with us.

Back in the cities, transient individuals, students, squatters, and those looking to save money made use of discarded furniture left on the streets. In New York City, one- and two-family homes were being turned into illegal boarding houses or carved up into studio apartments. Discarded mattresses were being picked up, refurbished, and resold with bed bugs inside. Individuals didn't know they had bed bugs and allowed infestations to go unchecked for months. Doctors couldn't identify the bites; they hadn't been seen in forty years.

Today, because of how quickly bed bugs become resistant to families of chemicals, we don't have a great variety of chemical options that allow us to treat for bed bugs. Most of today's products are synthetic pyrethrins or also known as pyrethroids. Other products are available but may be more expensive or work slower. That is why the IPM multipronged approach has become so important and why other methods such as heat or cold are being utilized.

All these factors were the setting for the new century to come—and it came with a bang!

CHAPTER 2

BIOLOGY OF
BED BUGS

"Bed bug" is two separate words and is based on the way entomologists classify insects. We separate the words to signify the insect belongs to "the order" of "the bug." A ladybug, as an entomologist knows, is not a lady or a true bug. The ladybug is actually a beetle. We classify insect using Linnaeus's system of classifying animals. True bugs like the bed bug are classified under the order known as Hemiptera. The bed bug is of a suborder of Hemiptera called Heteroptera.

Heteroptera, known as true bugs, are a diverse group (suborder) of about seventy-five families and thirty-eight thousand species (Schuh and Slater 1995). These insects have a segmented beak or proboscis which arises from the front of their heads and projects backwards under the head area. The forewings or hemelytra overlap one another at their tips when they are not being used in flight (Mallis 1997). This same forewing is thicker at the basal portion and more membranous at the distal tip. This gave the true bugs their name "Hemi," meaning half, and "ptera," referring to the wings. True bugs have a gradual metamorphosis, piercing-sucking mouthparts, and diverse lifestyles. Most are terrestrial; some aquatic or riparian; many are plant feeders, others seed and sap feeders; some are predators, and a few are ectoparasites (Mallis1997). Ectoparasites are animals that feed on other animals but do not live on them. They will leave the animal to mate, lay eggs, and complete their lifecycles.

Within this order we find the family known as Cimicidae, the bed bugs. This family consists of the bed bug, bat bug, and several bird bugs. All of them look very similar to each other. The members of this family are small, oval, dorsoventrally flattened with short hemelytra (wing pads). They are parasites of mammals and birds. They have a rostrum or proboscis that lies in a ventral groove. The legs distal tarsi are three-jointed. Their color is mahogany brown (hence the nickname "mahogany flats" or "red coats"), and measure about 1/5 inch or 5 mm in length. They also measure 1/8 inch or 3 mm across. They do not have functional wings therefore they cannot fly.

The species found in the United States are as follows:

SPECIES	HOST	DISTRIBUTION
Cimex lectularis Common bed bug	Human, bats, poultry, pigeons, pets, lab animals	**All 50 states and many countries around the world. Pandemic**
Cimex adjunctus Barber Eastern bat bug	Human, bats, poultry	**More than 20 states**
Cimex hempipterus (F.) Tropical bed bug	Human, bats, poultry	**Fla., Puerto Rico, occasionally NY and other states**
Orithocaris pallidus Usinger	Poultry, birds	**Fla., Ga., Brazil**
Haematosiphon indorus (Duges) Poultry bug	Poultry, owls	**Ariz., Calif., Kan., Okla, N.M., Texas, Mexico**
Cimex pilosellus (Horvath) Western bat bug	Bats	**At least 8 states and parts of Canada**
Cimex brevis Usinger and Ueshima	Bats	**Ill., Mich., Minn., Quebec, Alberta**
Cimex incrassatus Usinger and Ueshima	Bats	**South Western States, Mexico, Guatemala**

SPECIES	HOST	DISTRIBUTION
Cimex antennatus Usinger and Ueshima	Bats	**Calif., Nev.**
Cimex latipennis Usinger and Ueshima	Bats	**Calif., Idaho, Mon., Ore.**
Princimex cavenis Barber	Bats	**Texas, Mexico,Guatemala**
Hespericimex coloradensis List	Purple Martin and woodpecker nests	**Calif., Colo., N.D. Ore., British Columbia, Mexico**
Hespericimex sonorenus Ryckman	Purple Martin and wood pecker nests	**Ariz., Mexico**
Cimexopsis nyctalis List Chimney swift bug	Chimney swift	**Over 15 states**
Synxenodemus comosus List	White-throated swift	**Calif., Nev.**
Oeciacus vicarious Horvath Swallow bug	Swallows	**10 states and Canada**

From Henry and Froeschner 1988 and Mallis 1997

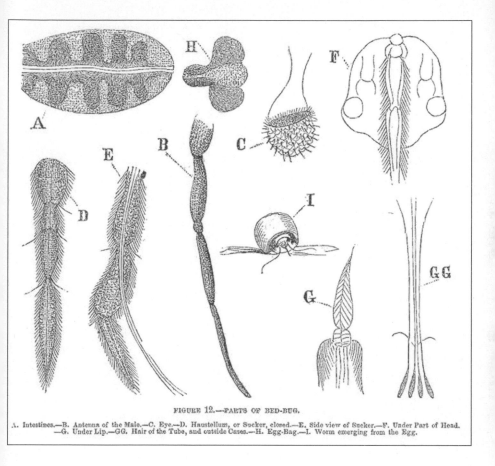

FIGURE 12.—PARTS OF BED-BUG.

A. Intestines.—B. Antenna of the Male.—C. Eye.—D. Haustellum, or Sucker, closed.—E. Side view of Sucker.—F. Under Part of Head.
—G. Under Lip.—GG. Hair of the Tube, and outside Cases.—H. Egg-Bag.—I. Worm emerging from the Egg.

Description and Biology

When describing a bed bug we say that the adult is broadly oval and dorsoventrally flat with small hemelytra (short wing pads). They have a three-segment beak or proboscis, which they use to feed on mammals. The piercing-sucking mouthparts are not like that of the mosquitoes.

The labium is the outer portion of the proboscis. Within is the mandibular stylet covering the maxillary stylet, which consists of the food canal and the salivary duct. Only the mandibular and maxillary stylets penetrate into the skin in search of the capillaries containing the blood meal. The mandibular stylet is provided with barbs which perform a sawing action (Mallis 1964). The proboscis is located at the front of the head. Also located on the head are the four-segment setaceous antennae. Bed bugs have a pair of compound eyes with no ocelli. Ocelli are simple eyes to detect light. The head contains the eyes.

The bed bug is covered with short golden hairs all over its body. The thorax or middle section of the bed bug is where the legs are attached. The vestiges of wings, in the form of wing pads, are found on the thorax. The wings are not functional, therefore bed bugs they cannot fly.

The abdomen or last segment contains the digestion system and the reproductive system.

The male's penis is located at the tip, giving the males a more pointed end. The female has a small nicklike cleft

Piercing-sucking mouth

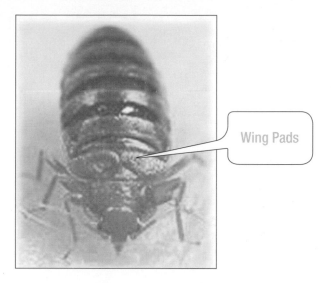

Wing Pads

at the posterior margin of the fourth apparent abdominal segment, which marks the opening of the copulatory pouch. Sex occurs when the male climbs on the female's back and wraps his abdomen around her and enters this nicklike cleft in traumatic fashion, hence the term *traumatic insemination*.

The male's reproductive organ actually pierces the cuticle of the female's abdomen and injects sperm through the wound, outside of the reproductive tract (Usinger 1966)

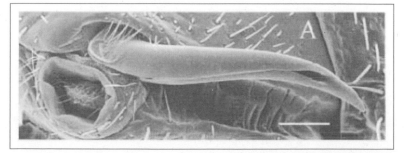

PHOTO BY: *Stutt and Siva-Jothy 2001*
This is a picture of the male's reproductive organ

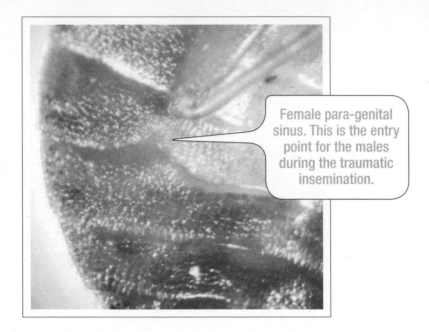

Female para-genital sinus. This is the entry point for the males during the traumatic insemination.

The eggs are about ¹⁄₂₅ inch or 1 mm long, white or creamy white, elongated, and have a slightly bowed shape. The female glues them onto a surface, which a vacuum cannot then pick up. There is a lid on one end of the egg that pops open and allows the newborn nymph, the first instar

PHOTO FROM
bed bugsnewyorkcity.com

This is a picture of a cluster of eggs.

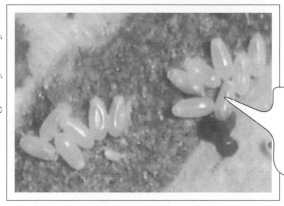

Newly hatched egg; notice where the bed bug emerged from.

Another picture of eggs cemented or glued to the wood.

to emerge (the first instar is the name given to this stage in the bed bug lifecycle). Each of the young stages are given a numerical instar. This allows us to track the growth stage with accuracy. The female usually lays her eggs in small, protected crevices. They can be seen against a dark surface, usually in clusters. The female will lay one to eight eggs at a time. The female will lay up to five hundred eggs in her lifetime. I have seen as many as eight eggs laid in one night. It will take six to ten days for the first eggs to hatch.

This is a newly hatched egg with the lid popped off.

Some eggs may take as long as twenty-one days to hatch. Only when temperature fall below 55.4°F/13°C or above 98.6°F/37°C will the eggs fail to hatch (Johnson 1940).

Once the nymph or first instar emerges out of the egg by forcing the lid open, it will be white or tan in color.

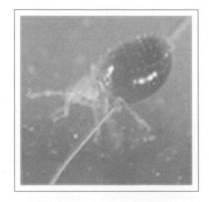

At this point it requires a blood meal. Once it has its first meal, it will go into hiding. Its color is now purple or red.

It will then molt and enter its second instar. This takes place over the period of a week. There will be a total of five instars or growth stages, each taking a week to complete under optimal conditions. Between each instar the nymph is required to have a blood meal in order to have the nutrients it requires to complete the molt.

This is a great picture showing the eggs on the left and each of the five stages of growth a bed bug goes through.

Once maturity is reached, the male bed bug seeks out a female to mate with. The male is capable of mating with several females over a twenty-four-hour period.

The female rarely lays eggs without a blood meal first. Once she has mated and has received enough sperm, she will migrate away from all males to lay her eggs.

Although bed bugs will commonly feed once a week, they can go a very long time without a blood meal. It's been proven that bed bugs may live more than one and a half years without a blood meal. In fact, Johnson in 1940 reported that a female bed bug had lived more than 560 days without food at a constant temperature of 44.6°F/7.2°C and 90 percent humidity.

So are humans the only creatures the common bed bug will feed on? No! They'll feed on many different mammals to survive. Your pets are vulnerable—this includes dogs, cats, birds, and livestock. One of the theories is that today's bed bug infestation started from bed-bug-carrying swallows infesting chicken coops. These same chickens were sent to slaughter throughout the country with the bed bugs going for a ride. Again there are many other reasons why the increase in bed bug reports is taking place. Just be aware that you are not the only victim.

Physical Reactions

The bites are not felt at the time of feeding. Bed bugs have perfected the anesthetic necessary to feed for approximately *ten minutes* without being detected. The reactions from the bite vary from person to person. Some individuals never have a reaction. Others will develop itching and small welts at the site of the bite. Still others will notice bites along a straight line. This is because the bed bugs search for the small blood vessels under the skin and follow them as they feed. In the worst cases, boils may occur as a severe allergic reaction. The reaction may happen quickly within several hours, or days later. In some cases, individuals still think they are getting bitten after extermination treatment because they are still scratching an old bite from days ago that only recently reacted. This can occur as many as two to four days later. My personal reaction to mosquito bites is to scratch until I have a good-sized

PHOTO BY *Dr. Philip Koehler*

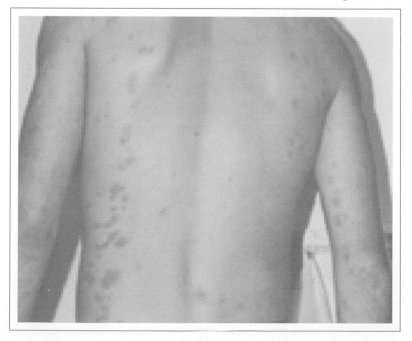

scab. It just feels so good to scratch it, doesn't it? Remember, this is not good since it could lead to infection.

Notice the bite marks forming a line.

Immediate immune reactions may appear from one to twenty-four hours after a given bite and may last one to two days, but delayed immune reactions usually first appear one to three days after a bite and may last two to five days (Fiengold, Benjamin, and Michaeli 1968).

Just like cockroaches, bed bugs produce allergens that may lead to bronchial asthma. Also noted is that numerous routine bites can contribute to anemia and may even make a person more susceptible to common disease (Unsinger 1966).

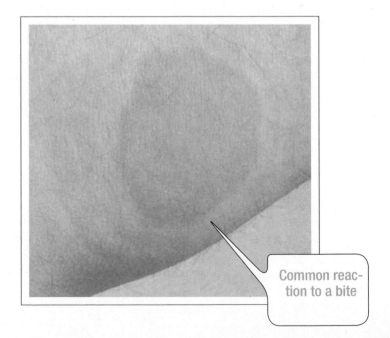

Common reaction to a bite

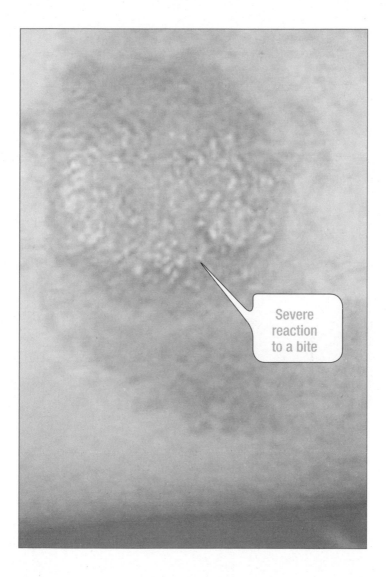

CHAPTER 3

GUIDE TO PREVENTION

Prevention takes vigilance. The more that you are aware of your surroundings, the less likely you are to accidently pick up bed bugs. Remember that bed bugs are fantastic hitchhikers.

- When you travel on public transportation, examine the seat before sitting down.

- When you get off again, give yourself a quick once over to check for any hitchhikers. Any bag, purse, or package you travel with—examine it carefully. Inspect the public bench before sitting down for lunch or a snack.

- Bring a small LED flashlight with you to the movie theater to inspect the seat and the area around you. Please remember to be courteous to others around you while performing your inspection.

- At a restaurant, club, or catering hall, examine your coat after retrieving it from the coat room. Examine the pockets and seams carefully.

- Keep your work environment organized and clean. Inspect every day for signs of bed bugs. Report any findings quickly to your supervisor.

- Inspect your locker at work or at the gym before placing any items inside. Inspect them again after removing the items. Again, report any findings quickly to maintenance or management.

- At home, set up a safe zone; this is an area you place your belongings when you first arrive at home. Inspect the items very carefully since this is the last time you have a chance to prevent them from getting into your home. If you miss it here, then the bed bugs get in.

- Launder your clothing on a regular basis. Don't wait an entire month; if possible, do it weekly at the very least.

- Make use of a passive detection system such as Climb-ups on your bed posts to monitor for bed bugs trying to make their way up on your beds.

- Take off bed skirts—just don't use them. Don't have anything on your bed that makes contact with the floor. Only the bed post should make contact. Keep the bed away from the wall by several inches. When cleaning the home, remember to clean behind the bed regularly.

- Vacuum!

When Traveling

When traveling, try and pack as light as possible. Vacuum-packed bags are a great investment as they remove as much of the air as possible while sealing and protecting your clothing. Also remember—it's easier to spot bed bugs on light-colored clothing.

When you arrive at your destination, prepare to inspect everything. Carry a small LED flashlight. You may be able to carry a small can of insecticide flushing agent, but I don't recommend it—it's a hassle to get through airport security and is not the most effective method of prevention. Place the luggage on a flat clean surface and use the flashlight to inspect your luggage as you open it. Remove each item carefully. Once the inspection is complete, put everything back. Do not use the drawers or closet if possible. If you are staying for an extended time inspect the drawers and closet before placing any items inside. Inspect these areas every day that you stay in the room. This is a must. Remember, someone will be entering the room on a daily basis to clean. The housekeeper is visiting other rooms prior to yours and may transport bed bugs into your room at any time. Before you depart, inspect the entire room one last time.

Inspect your luggage one last time prior to packing. Inspect each item. Once the luggage is filled, place by the door or in the hallway.

If at any time you find evidence of bed bugs, report it to management. Keep a small notebook with you to record

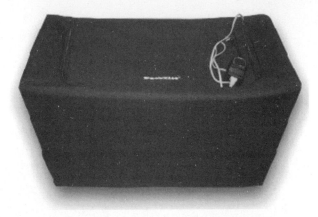

This is a small heat chamber for carry-on luggage and small items such as books and shoes.

dates and times of your inspection and findings. This will help everyone in pinning down how and when the bed bugs were transported into the room.

When you arrive home, inspect everything inside in your safe zone—be it a basement entrance, front hallway, or mud room. Some items may be placed inside a small bag that heats them specifically for the purpose of killing bed bugs. The device is called PackTite.

Your carry-on luggage should fit right inside—just plug it in and heat for several hours. This will kill all stages of the bed bug including the eggs.

If this all sounds like paranoia, then you've never experienced the nightmare of having bed bugs. Trust me—a little vigilance goes a long way.

Visitors

This is one area where we forget ourselves. When someone comes into our home-they bring bags or purses and in the cooler months-coats or jackets. We place these items in our closets or on our beds—and now we have bed bugs! Obviously, we need to be good hosts and not insult our guests, but we need to protect our home at the same time. As they offer you their coats, give them a visual inspection and try to create a safe zone. Perhaps you can purchase a coat rack or reserve a closet that you use only for guests. A bed or bedroom is a last resort, for obvious reasons.

Inspect each coat briefly prior to returning them to their owners. You don't want them to blame you for a bed bug brought into their home. It may not be your fault, but if they pick it up at *your* party, they will believe it came from *you*. Finally, inspect the room the coats were kept in. Inspect it from top to bottom.

Assistant Services

If you require assistant service personnel to come to your home (medical personnel, meals on wheels, dog walkers, etc.), provide them with a container for their belongings. This container should seal shut. This will provide two services—one, it will reduce the possibility of them bringing in bed bugs, or if you have them, it will prevent them from taking them home. Once more, remember, these individuals may be visiting several homes a day. They may encounter someone who is incapable of taking care of a bed bug infestation or who is unaware they have an infestation.

If you believe someone has brought bed bugs into your home, you must immediately call the service manager and report the situation before others become infested.

Deliveries

Deliveries of furniture or mattresses are one of the easiest ways that bed bugs are transported into a home. Many mattress companies will remove your old mattress at no cost. Great! Except that the old mattresses and your new mattress get transported in the same trucks. So before the mattress is taken off the vehicle, ask to inspect it. If you see bed bugs, refuse the delivery. Once merchandise is off the truck and in your home, it is usually your problem. By then, it is too late and the bed bugs will start to migrate off the delivered item and into your home.

Used Furniture

Used furniture may be of better quality than many of today's more disposable pieces. Where you buy your vintage furniture and how it's transported may make a difference. Browse through a thrift shop and inspect it at the same time. A well-kept shop means that the proprietors care about the merchandise. Ask if they have their own delivery personnel or if they use a privately owned trucking company. Either way you are better off picking up the piece yourself than using their service. If you must use theirs, see if they will let you inspect the vehicles that will make the delivery. This is unusual, but it will prevent dealing with an infestation in your home. If they say no, shop elsewhere or insist on curbside inspection prior to the delivery being brought into your home.

Co-ops, Condos, and Multiple Dwellings

The rules are different for rental apartments and cooperatives than they are for condominiums—it's up to you to find out your rights for your particular living situation. Both the rentals and cooperatives fall under the lease term agreements. These agreements in many cases provide the requirement as to who is responsible for any pest infestations. Case law throughout the last century has made it clear that the *owner* or *management* in most cases is responsible for the treatment or control of any pest within the dwelling.

The following is a condensed account of a recent court decision from 2004 where a tenant was taken to court by his landlord. The tenant had stopped paying his rent after the bed bug problem in his studio apartment became so severe that he was sleeping on a metal cot at night. Keeping up with recent court decisions is an excellent way for tenants and landlord to educate themselves about their rights.

New York City Housing court Decisions

Housing court Decision Summaries
Property Management X v. John Doe
Jun. 21, 2004

Trial court:
Civil Housing court, New York County

Type of Action or Proceeding:
Nonpayment Proceeding - Warranty of Habitability

Issues/Legal Principles:
court awarded tenant a 45 percent abatement for infestation of bed bugs upon consideration of the size of the premises, the severity of the infestation, landlord's diligent effort to eradicate the condition, and the continued, although limited, use of the premises by tenant.

Summary:
Tenant withheld rent, alleging landlord's breach of warranty of habitability as a result of an unabated bed bug infestation. Landlord did not deny the existence or extent of the condition. However, landlord argued tenant is not entitled to an

abatement as a diligent effort has been taken to eradicate the condition.

The court held that an abatement based upon the implied warranty of habitability protects only against conditions that materially affect the health and safety of tenants or deficiencies that in the eyes of a reasonable person, deprive the tenant of essential functions which a residence is expected to provide. The court ruled that "there can be no doubt that the presence of the bed bugs in the premises satisfies this criteria for an abatement." Accordingly, the court determined that the only remaining issue was the diminution in value of the subject premises.

The court noted that bed bugs, unlike rodents, feed "upon one's blood . . . and turns what is supposed to be bed rest or sleep into a hellish experience." As a result, the precedential value of prior abatements awarded for the existence of "vermin" are of limited value. The court further noted that the only reported cases involving bed bugs come from the early 1900s and predate the warranty of habitability.

In determining the amount of abatement, the court noted that it must be mindful that the condition may not be attributable to a landlord, and that the landlord did attempt multiple exterminations, to little or no avail. The court recognized that extermination is a difficult process due to the resiliency of bed bugs. The court further considered that tenant never actually vacated the subject premises as a result of this condition. Moreover, the court held that an abatement award must factor in the extent of which the premises could be occupied for the purposes of eating, bathing, and other residential functions.

In reaching its decision, the court considered "small size of the premises, the severity of the infestation, landlord's diligent effort to eradicate the condition, and the continued, although limited, use of the premises by tenant and held that a 45 percent abatement for the period in question was warranted.

OPINION OF THE COURT

Petitioner, "Property Manager X," commenced this nonpayment proceeding against respondent, "John Doe," seeking unpaid rents for "Property X," New York, New York (premises). Respondent interposed a breach of warranty of habitability defense, stemming largely from the presence of bed bugs in the premises.

The trial was held on April 22, 2004. After considering the credible evidence and testimony at trial, the court makes[2] the following findings of fact and conclusions of law:

The parties stipulated to most of petitioner's prima facie case. Petitioner is the owner and landlord of the premises, which is a rent-stabilized apartment in a multiple dwelling, duly registered in both respects. Respondent is in possession of the premises pursuant to a written lease commencing April 1, 2003, and the monthly rent is currently $1,025. As stipulated by the parties, the sum of $6,550 is unpaid through April 30, 2004.

The premise is a studio apartment with a sleeping loft raised on the brick wall on one side of the studio room with bathroom facilities within the premises on the other. Respondent slept in the loft bed until he realized the premises was infested with bed bugs when in the end of June 2003, he saw a posting (respondent's exhibit B-1) in the lobby of the building which read:

ATTENTION TENANTS PLEASE BE ADVISED THAT THE EXTERMINATOR WILL BE IN THE BUILDING ON SATURDAY AUGUST 2ND BETWEEN 9AM AND 2PM FOR A SPECIAL SERVICE FOR THE BED BUGS. PLEASE REMOVE ALL SHEETS AND PILLOWCASES FROM YOUR BEDS. PLACE ALL DIRTY CLOTHING IN BAGS TO HAVE IT CLEANED. PULL ALL

BOOKSHELVES AND OTHER FIXTURES AWAY FROM THE WALLS FOR BETTER ACCESS TO THOSE AREAS . . ."

Upon reading this posting, respondent realized the cause of the hundreds of bite marks he had noticed on his body since mid-June 2003 and why he was often startled awake many nights during this period—bed bugs.

Over the next few months, respondent employed four methods to attempt a restful night of sleep—none of which proved effective. First, he threw out his bed and all his bedding and slept on the floor after placing towels on the floor. He quickly realized this method was useless as he was still bitten hundreds of times. Next, he put plastic sheeting on the floor in the sleeping area he prepared. This method proved just as useless. In the third week of August, he bought an inflatable mattress to sleep upon. Besides the mattress requiring reinflation at least once during the night, the mattress was unacceptable as bed bugs still preyed upon his skin. Finally, since mid-September 2003, respondent has been sleeping on a metal cot with a wire mesh covering (respondent's exhibit D). This appeared to stop the biting of the bed bugs, but as demonstrated in the courtroom, no real comfort was possible in this less than six-foot metal cot.

For the period July 2003 through December 2003, respondent saw bed bugs on a regular basis. Respondent found bed bugs on his couch as late as December 2003. Respondent testified that he threw out a couch containing bed bug nests, an armoire, a shelf, books, drapes, towels, linens, and clothes. Respondent testified that he threw out everything except family heirlooms.

Respondent related a story about his Christmas holiday in December 2003 at his family's home in Massachusetts. He had to enter the family home through the basement, take off all his clothes, and place them in a plastic bag and then seal the bag with duct tape. He then took a hot shower for a half hour and was required to wear his father's clothes all weekend to make sure he did not bring any of the nymphs into his parents' home.

Petitioner had notice of the bed bug infestation since June 2003, according to the building's management. Petitioner's then exterminator established an attack plan to combat the bed bugs. It was in essence:

"All sheets, quilts, comforters and pillowcases to be removed from the beds and washed using hot water and detergent. All nightstands, bureaus, dressers, and closets to be emptied and all furniture and stored items to be moved away from the walls. Once this criteria was met, the exterminators could begin treatment.

"The treatment entailed spraying the mattresses, box springs and bedframes with products labeled for that application to target the bed bugs. Walls in the bedroom and living rooms were to be drilled and dust injected in the void areas. Baseboards, crack and crevices throughout the apartment were to be injected with aerosol products to flush out the bed bugs. The exterminator was to check outlets, picture frames, dressers and all furniture."[1]

The exterminator's report indicates that bed bugs are tenacious and adapt very well to their environment and can go a whole year without feeding. They can migrate to other apartments quickly through the walls on the interior and exterior. Bed bugs can go from endemic to epidemic if not handled properly (*see* respondent's exhibit A). The exterminator had anticipated two extermination treatments, along with sealing of the cracks in each apartment, to control the bed bug outbreak in the building which affected nearly nine of the sixty apartments in the building. The infestation

---

[1]   The parties stipulated that the methodology to combat the bed bugs in respondent's exhibit A was an effective method.

seemed to be clustered in a specific area of the building. Each extermination was expected to last two to three months.

Petitioner chose to adopt the methodology in the report to combat the bed bugs as suggested by his exterminators (respondent's exhibit A). However, in attempting to eradicate the bed bug infestation in the premises, the exterminators ended up exterminating in the premises on five occasions in the year 2003 starting in June 2003.

In addition to the bed bugs, respondent also complained to petitioner concerning the condition of the shower stall and the kitchen unit shortly after he moved into the premises. For three weeks in January 2004, three of petitioner's workers labored in the premises to correct the conditions. Petitioner's workers removed the old shower stall unit and installed a bathtub (respondent's exhibit E-3) which leaked after installation and caused damage to the studio room floor (respondent's exhibit E-4). To date, there is a maze of piping from the kitchen area to the newly installed bathtub.

The court finds the condition of bed bugs in the building generally was known to petitioner early in June 2003 and with respect to the premises particularly in late June 2003 when respondent informed petitioner. An abatement based upon the implied warranty of habitability pursuant to Real Property Law § 235-b protects only against conditions that materially affect the health and safety of tenants or deficiencies that in the eyes of a reasonable person deprive the tenant of those essential functions which a residence is expected to provide. (*Solow v Wellner*, 86 NY2d 582 [1995], quoting *Park W. Mgt. Corp. v Mitchell*, 47 NY2d 316 [1979].) Respondent showed through his graphic testimony that the bed bug infestation impacted or affected his health, safety and welfare and use of the premises. There can be no doubt that the presence of the bed bugs in the premises satisfies the above criteria for an abatement under these set of facts.

It is now for the court, in an apparent case of first impression involving warranty of habitability due to bed bugs, to determine the diminution in value of the premises. Although bed bugs are classified as vermin, they are unlike the more common situation of vermin such as mice and roaches, which although offensive, do not have the effect on one's life as bed bugs do, feeding upon one's blood in hoards, nightly turning what is supposed to be bed rest or sleep into a hellish experience. Therefore, the cases involving abatements for "vermin" (i.e., mice and roaches) are of limited precedential value for the court in fashioning an appropriate abatement.

The only reported cases involving bed bugs which the court was able to find come from the early 1900s and predate warranty of habitability. These early cases revolve around whether the presence of the bed bugs constituted a constructive eviction. The cases turn on the severity of the infestation.[2]

The court is mindful that with time, the prevalence of cases in which bed bugs are involved is sure to increase to an epidemic as the foothold the bed bugs have obtained in the urban setting of the city of New York grows ever larger. However, in fixing what is a proper abatement, the

---

[2] *Jacobs v. Morand*, 59 Misc 200 (App Term, 1st Dept 1908) (premises overrun by bed bugs, making it inconvenient and untenable does, not constitute a constructive eviction); *Streep v. Simpson*, 80 Misc 666 (App Term, 2d Dept 1913) (where bed bugs constituted an insufferable nuisance, whose presence is nowise attributable to the tenant, causing substantial discomfort and severe inconvenience amounting to an intolerable state, the tenant was constructively evicted); *Michtom v. Miller*, 178 NYS 395 (App Term, 1st Dept 1919) (presence of bed bugs constituted mere annoyance); *Hancock Constr. Co. v. Bassinger*, 198 NYS 614 (App Term, 1st Dept 1923) (aggravated condition of bed bugs so numerous they could not be exterminated, constituted constructive eviction).

court is also mindful that the condition may not be attributable to a landlord, and that the landlord may attempt multiple exterminations to little or no avail due the resiliency of bed bugs from eradication.

In this case, the bed bugs did not constitute mere annoyance, but constituted an intolerable condition, notwithstanding the landlord's efforts to exterminate them. Respondent, however, did not vacate the premises or raise the defense of constructive eviction. In circumstances as in this case where a landlord has tried repeatedly to exterminate but the infestation is so overwhelming that although the tenant may have been relieved of his obligation to pay rent had he vacated, as he did not, equity requires the court take into account the purposes for which the premises was still being utilized by respondent. Stated differently, the court looks to what essential functions or uses respondent still used the premises notwithstanding the bed bugs.

Clearly one essential function of a residence is a place to sleep, but it is not the only function. Respondent continued to use the premises for shelter, eating, bathing and for work purposes which are other essential functions, or activities a premises is utilized. This in no way diminishes what respondent went through; however, whatever benefit was still being derived by respondent from the premises is fair to take into consideration in determining the abatement.

Based upon the small size of the premises, the severity of the bed bug infestation, the effect the infestation had on respondent, the lack of showing petitioner's efforts to eradicate the bed bugs on a building-wide scale, petitioner's diligent efforts to eradicate the bed bugs and the use respondent continued to make of the premises, the court finds an abatement of 45 percent commencing July 1, 2003 (date rent first sought in the petition) through December 31, 2003 to be appropriate (6 × $1,025 × 45 percent = $2,767.50). Respondent is granted an additional abatement in the sum of $150 for the other conditions complained of.

There was no testimony that any bed bugs were seen or present after December 2003. Presumably the multiple exterminations have finally turned the tide, and hopefully rendered the premises bed bug free. Although respondent continues to curtail his full use of the premises by sleeping on the metal cot rather than buy another bed for fear of reinfestation, there was no showing or testimony by a qualified expert that this is a potential risk due to a latency period before one can determine whether the eradication is successful, this precaution adopted by respondent on his own cannot serve for the court to grant a continuing abatement after December 31, 2003.

Accordingly, final judgment of possession in petitioner's favor in the sum of $3,632.50 ($6,550 less abatements of $2,767.50 and $150) representing unpaid rents less abatement through April 30, 2003.

Resource: www.tenant.net

As you see, the courts are taking bed bugs very seriously. Tenants cannot live in bed bug-infested conditions, and ignoring bed bug infestations can ultimately cause a tremendous loss of revenue for landlords and property managers. They must find ways to curb the infestations. One potential solution can be to inspect empty apartments and have reports written by an inspector. Currently banks require inspection of wood-destroying insects when mortgages are required—this ensures the banks or mortgage companies that the home is free or protected against wood destroying insects or organisms. The same may eventually apply for bed bugs. If an inspector clears an apartment then it can be rented or a lease given. Another inspection should be required one month after occupancy. This should be written into the lease. If the apartment clears, then the landlord has provided an inexpensive way of reducing the chances that bed bugs are brought into the building. If an infestation is found, then it is found in the early stages and can be eliminated before it infests the rest of the building. This method also provides an added value service to the landlord. A landlord who cares to provide these inspections will likely attract better tenants as well.

These are all possibilities that may become standard practice in the future; however, any landlord or prospective tenant thinking about this process of inspection before and after occupancy should consult a lease attorney for advice.

Exclusion

"Pest proofing" or exclusion is one aspect of IPM which the general public comprehends the least. We in the pest management field spend lots of valuable time trying to explain to individuals the importance of changing our environment. This is so that what we term as pests (unwanted plants, fungi, or animals) don't compete, damage, or endanger us. Sealing the small holes around a pipe appears to be nonsense, but this little task prevents all sorts of pests from entering your home environment. Access under and around doors allows mice. Flies, roaches, ground beetle, moths, and many other types of unwanted animals also gain entrance into or places of work and homes through doors and windows.

But what does exclusion do for us when it comes to bed bugs? Bed bugs have piercing and sucking mouth parts which makes them incapable of chewing. The tarsi or toes are also incapable of clawing through even the very thin layer of sealant, unbroken paper, or cloth.

We need to prevent bed bugs from obtaining easy access to cracks and crevices along baseboards and trim work in our homes. Sealing these areas will allows us to see the bed bugs faster and therefore treat the problem more quickly.

So what kinds of materials should we be using? There is good old plaster of paris for the older homes, silicon caulking, and other types of caulking materials at the local hardware stores. Each material is a tool, and each job site is different.

We may have exactly the same home but in different environments. One home may be located in a cold, wet part of the country while the other is exposed to dry, hot climates. The materials must be compatible with the environment so that they can last. A material that becomes hard and brittle may in itself create small cracks and crevices for bed bugs to live. A material used around windows which cools and heats several times in a day needs to be pliable, to expand and contract.

If bed bugs are sealed into a void, wall, or other area, even if they live for a year they will have no access to the rest of the bed bug population or food source (you)—they will eventually die.

How about "excluding" bed bugs from our stuff? Our clothing may be sealed in plastic bags and similarly tightly-sealed containers which will greatly reduce the ability of the bed bug to gain access to food and other harboring places.

Protect-A-Bed mattress encasement

Our mattresses can and should be covered with commercial mattress encasements. One of the very few I recommend are the Protect-A-Bed mattress and box spring covers. There are covers for pillows as well. This company has made it a point of creating a mattress encasement which is easy to put on and won't rip or tear. The zipper is of a special size which will keep nymphs from escaping between the teeth.

Bed Bug Detection Methods

Even with the best prevention methods, you may still get bed bugs. If you suspect you have them there are a few ways of finding out for sure before enlisting the help of a pest management company. There are two types of detection systems: passive and active. The passive systems are less expensive and readily available. The active systems are still being developed and very costly.

During the 2009 Entomological Society of America meeting in Indianapolis, one of the sessions examined the locomotion of bed bugs over several types of surfaces. Smooth plastic with a thin layer of talcum dust proved to be the most difficult surface for bed bugs to move across. So one product, Climb-ups has proven to be an inexpensive passive system for detecting bed bugs. It looks like a round dish that is place under each of the bed post. When bed bugs try to climb up the side of the dish they fall into a pit which contains a small amount of dust. This dust then prevents the bed bugs from escaping.

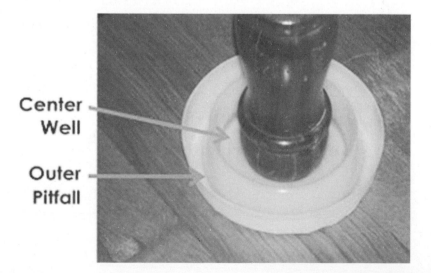

Center Well

Outer Pitfall

Another passive method is a glue-monitoring device that traps wandering bed bugs. This device takes advantage of bed bugs' ability to hide in small crevices—you can slide the trap under the bed or into corners where they might be hiding. A plain mouse glue board will do—this catches bed bugs (and mice) using glue that bonds on contact. Now on the market are glue boards specifically geared towards bed bugs, which trick them into believing they've found a good home to hide in—usually this is done with a piece of corrugated cardboard attached to the bottom of the trap.

An active bed bug detection system will use heat and/or pheromone to attract bed bugs to the trap. Pheromones are a chemical means of communication for insects. In 2008 at the Entomologic Society of America annual meeting, one of the sessions introduced a study on bed bug pheromones. It found at least twelve different pheromones

Passive monitoring device with glue (top view)

Same passive device viewed from the side

involved in bed bugs' attraction to one another. These include sex pheromones and congregate pheromones. Congregate pheromones signal to other bed bugs where they are gathering to hangout. This may be for safety reasons. What the study found was that all the nymphs, unfertilized females, and male bed bugs would gather together. The one major drawback (for exterminators at least) was that the fertilized females would be repelled by those same pheromones. This means that any device using active pheromones to trap the bed bugs would have the potential of scattering pregnant females to other parts of a room. This is because of the way bed bugs have sex—the traumatic insemination. If the fertilized female gets too many punctures, she will lose her life, so she runs away.

Another active device is the use of CO_2 in the form of dry ice. The dry ice is placed inside a small thermos which in turn is placed on top of an upside down dog bowl. The sides of the dog bowl are lightly taped to allow bed bugs to climb up. The CO_2 attracts the bed bugs by simulating human breathing. A small amount of talc powder is placed in the bowl—the plastic surface and the talc prevent the bed bugs from escaping. When used correctly, this device will detect bed bugs within a week's time.

Bed Bug Dogs

Trained pest professionals are only able to detect *visible* signs of bed bugs with an accuracy rate of about 30 percent. Because bed bugs usually only come out at night, and like to hide inside walls, baseboards and under carpets, these areas are beyond the scope of a visual inspection. Because of canines' superior sniffing capabilities, they can detect bed bugs with up to 90 percent accuracy or better. Canines can service homes, condominiums, apartments, cooperative living and business units, office buildings, colleges, hotels and motels, local, state and federal buildings, nursing homes, hospitals, assisted living centers, furniture and mattress companies, cruise liners, bus companies, etc.

When enlisting the help of a bed bug-sniffing dog, there are a few things to consider. The dog may get distracted by other animals, toys, and smells from food in your home. Therefore it is best to pick up items such as toys, shoes, and stuffed animals and place them in a bag. Children and pets should be removed from the premises. All windows should be closed and air conditioners shut off. This is to prevent the odors that the dog is trying to detect from floating around the room and confusing the canine.

The client and Pest Management Professional should not play with the canine or distract it. This is a working animal. Allow the handler to do his or her job.

Pest Management Professionals may take hours inspecting and not find any bed bugs.

It will take only minutes to inspect an apartment. The handler may inspect the room or rooms several times to make sure the canine is doing its job. A good inspector will carry live bed bugs in a container to test the canine periodically.

If the canine "marks," it will help everyone involved in the preparation and treatment. This is because it will have narrowed down the area of infestation. The Pest Management Professional will spend more time in the area to make sure the infestation is eliminated.

Bed bug dogs are on average *90 percent accurate* in detecting bed bugs. The nose knows!

According to the Institute for Biological Detection Systems (IBDS), dogs have the following capabilities:

- **Sensitivity:** Can detect odors diluted to five hundred parts per trillion.

- **Discrimination:** Dogs can differentiate a target vapor from non-target vapors even at relatively high concentrations of non-target odors.

- **Odor Signatures:** Dogs are trained to detect only one or two of the target odors with the most abundant vapor compounds.

- **Multiple Odor Discriminations:** Dogs easily learn to differentiate between ten distinct odors.

Why Use a Bed Bug Dog?

- Less expensive
- Quicker and more accurate results

- Proven and trusted. "Man's best friend" has been used for years by military and law enforcement personnel for everything from search and rescue to drug detection.

- Greater peace of mind. If the dog doesn't find bed bugs you're probably safe from bed bugs.

The dog should be certified by a governing body overseeing that the proper training has taken place. One example is the National Entomology Scent Detection Canine Association (NESDCA) Dogs. NESDCA was founded by professionals in the pest control industry to ensure standardization and high standards for the training of these dogs. Many of the dogs are rescued from shelters before they are destroyed. From their website:

NESDCA is committed to:

- **Providing** entomology scent detection canine teams with an evaluation process to maintain the highest quality standards.

- **Improving the image** of entomology scent-detecting canine teams.

- **Educating consumers** about the benefits of using properly trained entomology scent-detecting dog teams in the process of locating and eradicating pest problems.

- **Contributing to and participating** in entomology-related research

CHAPTER 4

GUIDE TO
TREATMENTS

This guide to treatment is designed to help facilitate the preparation for someone who does have an infestation. Depending on the pest management company you hire, the preparation may vary. Some companies will provide preparation services. You may find the process overwhelming, and therefore might want to consider this option.

In the appendix I give a detailed guide on how to hire a pest management company. The basic version is this: hire someone who has been around for a while, certified, insured, has a preparation sheet, contract, and good customer service (you can often find reviews of a company online). The cost for bed bug work varies. In general, it should not cost less than $300 per room. It may cost as much as $5,000 to treat a house. This cost does not include discarding furniture, laundering, replacement furniture, physical or mental health cost, or your time.

Preparation for Treatment

Preparation for a bed bug treatment is akin to something in between spring cleaning and moving out. You will have to go through everything. Take this time to clean out the home. Throw out the items you haven't used in years and really don't need anymore. During this process, every precaution must be taken to ensure that you do not spread the infestation outside your home. The discarded items must be bagged to prevent the spread of the infestation to others inside your apartment building or well-intentioned neighbors who go through discarded items along the curbside trash. In most places, just like in NYC, once an item is placed on the curbside for garbage pickup, it is illegal for someone to take it. I have seen people use magic marker to write "bed bugs" or draw a skull and crossbones on any items they place curbside.

The following bullet points will help in the preparation:

- First, purchase clear garbage bags for the clothing that will need to be laundered. Remember that the bag used to transport the clothing *cannot* be reused to bring them back, therefore buy twice the amount needed to transport them.

- Some items may need to be dry-cleaned and then kept in sealed bags or containers for at least one month. The

reason to remain prepared is so that you don't have to go through the entire process and inconvenience again if you need to re-treat in a few weeks' time.

• Closets need to be emptied and accessible.

• The only kind of vacuum that should be used is one with a HEPA (high-efficient particulate air filter) to filter out particles as small as 0.3 microns. This is to prevent small insect parts from entering the air as allergens. Make sure that the bag is sealed and thrown out after each use.

• Bed linens *cannot* be treated with insecticides for safety reasons, therefore they will need to be laundered with the rest of your clothes.

- Pictures hanging on the walls will need to be taken down. Many Pest Management Professionals are reluctant to remove them from the wall for fear of damaging them. During the initial inspection, a review of treatment procedures concerning pictures, paintings, and other delicate items should be understood. If this is not done, then they may not get treated, and the bed bug infestation may return in short time.

- Stuffed animals, although cute, may harbor many bed bugs. These items should be placed in a dryer on high heat for at least ten minutes. They then should be stored in clear plastic bags for no less than one month. You may want to consider discarding these items if they don't hold sentimental value.

- Books, papers, phones, radios, TVs, shoes, and other items that cannot be laundered should be heat treated or fumigated. The Pest Management Professional should help you with this or provide you with a referral to someone who can. Although the technician will be moving items around the room, the pest management company is not responsible for *the preparation* prior to the service. That is a completely different service. Some pest management companies will perform this service for a much larger fee. It can cost as much as several thousand dollars just to prepare a home for treatment.

- The furniture in the home is going to be treated. Review with the inspector the type of treatment that will be used for each item. Night tables will be treated differently than a baby's crib. No insecticide should ever be used on the crib. Steam or freeze it. Fumigation is the only insecticidal option available because once treated no residual chemical is left on it. Nonresidual aerosols or liquid may stain the crib and carry inert ingredients that should not be applied to cribs for safety reasons.

PHOTO BY *Angel Avila*

The room will be taken apart during the treatment process.

- Mattresses, box springs, couches, chairs, and other furniture will be treated and should be free from blankets, bedding, pillows, etc. The Pest Management Professional will require some room to set up a safe zone. The PMP will be removing, in many cases, the cloth under the box spring and couches for treatment.

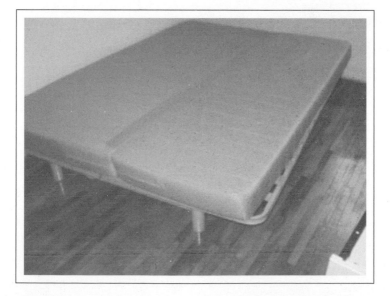

PHOTO BY *Angel Avila*

The cloth under the box spring will be removed in many cases.

PHOTO BY *Angel Avila*

PHOTO BY *Angel Avila*

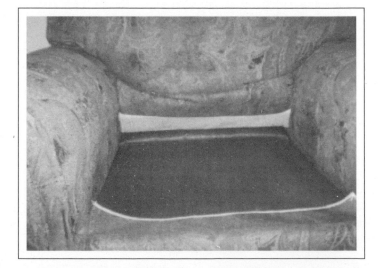

PHOTO BY *Angel Avila*

- Curtains will need to be removed and either laundered, dry-cleaned, or at least placed in the dryer on high heat for ten minutes. The items will need to be stored in clear plastic bags for a minimum of one month after treatment.

Rugs will need to be vacuumed and will be treated by the PMP.

PHOTO BY *Angel Avila*

- Move everything away from the walls to provide access
  to the baseboard molding and outlets.

- Outlet covers will be removed and replaced during treatment.

PHOTO BY *Angel Avila*

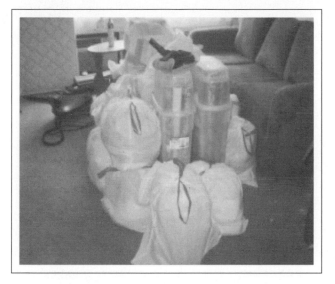

Place items in the center of the room.

Inspection

On the day of treatment, the same inspector or a technician will arrive at the home. Usually a team of two or more technicians will arrive. One will review your preparations. If this PMP determines that the preparation is done well, treatment will be provided. If the PMP determines that additional preparation is needed, they may reschedule the treatment. This may cost you more money to reschedule the service. So if you realize you need more time to prepare, call the pest management company before your appointment to avoid additional cost.

Some minor questions may arise while preparing so don't hesitate to call the pest management company and ask. Yes, you (or they) might feel that you are pestering them, but most companies are more than happy to make sure you are ready before they arrive. The pest management company does not want to reschedule or lose the work for that day. They want everything to go smoothly.

Creating a Safe Zone

The Pest Management Professional will create a safe zone in each room or a section of the home to move furniture to once treated. This helps them keep an organized treatment method and assures that every item that requires treatment is done. It also allows them to access parts of the walls and outlets. So please remember that some items will not be placed back after the treatment exactly where you had them originally. If this is a problem for you, review it with your PMP prior to treatment to avoid confusion and anger.

Products and Techniques

Use of Dusts

There are many types of insecticidal dust on the market. Different Pest Management Professionals prefer different types due to cost or other reasons. The dusts have been found to provide long-term residual effects and very quick kills.

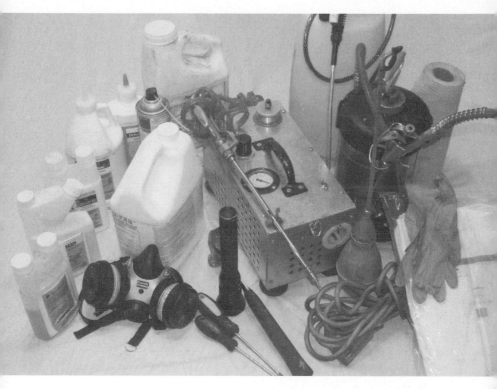

PHOTO BY *Angel Avila*

This is a picture of some of the products or techniques that may be used by a Pest Management Professional during a typical bed bug treatment. They may use one of these methods or a combination of these depending on which treatment option you chose with your PMP.

Although some label directions may say that you can use it liberally on floor surfaces, a good PMP will not treat in this manner. Treatment using dust formulations will be into voids or walls. This is why access to outlets is needed.

PHOTO BY *Angel Avila*

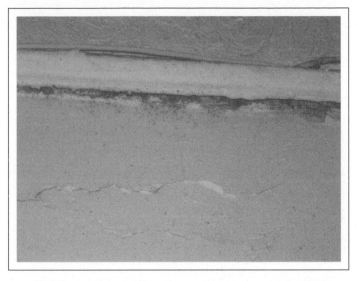

Moldings may also be removed in severe cases and treated into the voids.

PHOTO BY *Angel Avila*

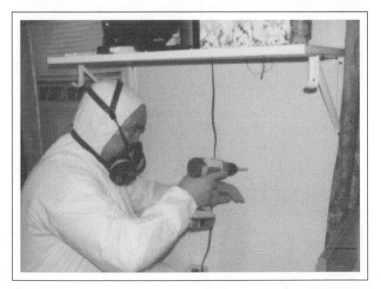

The covers will be removed and the dust, using a bulb dust (which is an application tool similar in appearance to a turkey baster), will be applied into the outlet and its surroundings.

Dust may also be used under some furniture and the box spring joints. The bed frame in some cases will be treated as well.

One of the most important areas of treatment is under the wall-to-wall carpets. The carpet edges need to be lifted and the dust inserted under the edges. This is very time-consuming.

In hotels, it is best to drill out behind the headboard bracket that hangs on the wall. This is an area where high percentages of bed bugs migrate from one room to the next.

Dusts are highly effective yet very messy. They leave visible evidence where treatment was performed. A good PMP will clean up, leaving very little outward evidence of the treatment. If a mess is left behind, call the company back and have them clean it up.

USE OF LIQUIDS

Liquids for bed bug control come in many varieties. Some are residuals and some are not. A good PMP will have different types for different circumstances. He may need a flushing agent to force the bed bugs out of an area, yet the product may not be good for long-term protection. A good PMP will have aerosols and may have a couple of compressed air sprayers. There was a time about ten years ago that many companies did away with their compressed air sprayers or B&Gs. They thought that the industry would no longer need them—I've had mine for over twenty years. My B&G never left my side.

One tank will contain the product to be used on mattresses, couches, and chairs. This is what's called "contact kill" and leaves very little residuals. When the liquid dries, dust may be used as a residual.

The other tank may have a combination of products that contain the residual with an insect growth regulator. The IGR is used to try to break the life cycle of a bed bug. They help by sterilizing the adults, preventing the eggs from hatching, and interrupting the ability of the bed bug to complete a molt from one instar to the next. It supplements the treatment that kills on contact to ensure

PHOTO BY *Angel Avila*

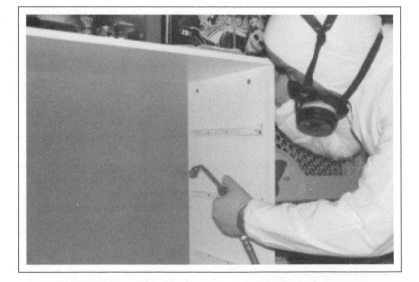

a long-term solution. The residual is applied using various strategies: crack and crevice, spot, or perimeter. The crack-and-crevice technique uses a pin spray to apply the product directly into small openings along baseboards, window frames, etc. This is faster than using the dust formulation, but doesn't last as long. Applying the product as a spot treatment or perimeter is when we spread the product evenly over a large area. This way as bed bugs travel over the residual, they will pick up enough of the product to kill them.

The problem as of this writing is that many of the liquid products currently in use today are from the same family of chemical known as pyrethroids. Bed bugs have now become highly resistant to many of these products, just as they have become resistant to other products in the past. Some bed bugs in the NYC area have been found to be three hundred times resistant to the common brands Suspend SC and Tempo SC. These products are still viable in that they are effective on some stages of the bed bug life cycle—just not all stages. When *combined* with other products, they can kill several stages of the instars or eggs.

Back in the 1980s, PMP rotated different families of pesticides. We were taught to use organophosphate for three months, switch to a pyrethroid for three months, and finally to a carbamate for three months. By rotating these families of chemicals, we didn't give the cockroaches time to develop resistance within a given population. If this is happening with bed bugs, we need to work in the same manner; however, this is far more difficult to do today since we no longer use organophosphate or carbamates in residential homes. We do have options like the brand name Phantom. Phantom belongs to a different chemical group which is nonrepellent but works more slowly than pyrethroids. Where pyrethroids are expected to kill bed bugs in minutes to hours, it may take Phantom up to ten days. Being one of the few products that has a residual after it dries, it is very useful in reducing the need for second or third treatments.

VACUUMS

Vacuums are an important tool for any Pest Management Professional using an IPM program. It helps in situations where regular pesticides cannot or should not be used—hospitals, food establishments, schools, and around cribs. In bed bug control vacuums, may be used to remove large infestations of nymphal and adult-stage bed bugs. Vacuums will *not* remove eggs since they are cemented or glued in place. Vacuuming also helps remove any debris which will help the products being used during a bed bug treatment to be more efficient. Vacuums should be used along the seams of furniture. The vacuum's attachments allow deep penetration into the folds of a sofa or couch. It is in these areas that bed bugs hide and breed. Don't just use any vacuum—use only ones with a high-efficiency particulate air (HEPA) filter.

A HEPA filter is a type of air filter that satisfies certain standards of efficiency set by the United States Department of Energy (DOE). HEPA filters, as defined by the DOE, remove at least 99.97 percent of airborne particles 0.3 micrometers (µm) in diameter. By removing such small particles, the filter prevents these potential allergens from releasing into the air. Allergens may cause asthma or other reactions in certain individuals. None of us want to solve one problem and cause another.

The use of a vacuum is like any other tool—in this case, it helps *prepare* the home for treatment and will also be used as part of the treatment process by your PMP. The vacuum is an important tool as it removes many of the bed bugs without the use of pesticides. Remember you must remove the bag *after each use* and seal it before discarding, so purchase several bags prior to vacuuming.

STEAM

Steam is an effective tool for treating a variety of surfaces. Steam may be used on a mattress along the seams and on other sensitive places where insecticides should never be used. The steamer's instructions must be followed, and the technician must be experienced in using the equipment. If the steamer's tip is too far away from the surface being treated, then the killing temperature will not be achieved. Any towel or rag being used to disperse the heat needs to be changed very often. This is because once it gets wet (and it will get wet), the temperature is not hot enough to kill the eggs or adult stages.

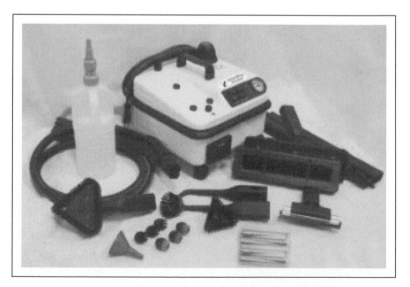

Complete steam unit used by Pest Management Professionals

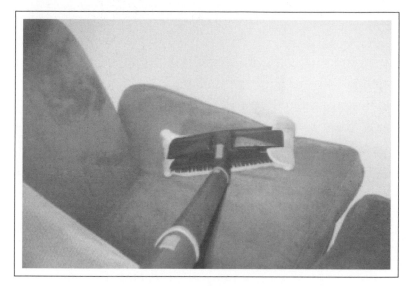

Steamer being used on a couch

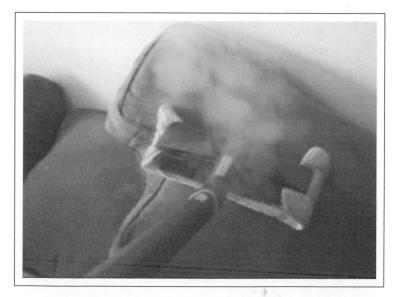

Steam temperatures may reach as high as 256°F.

HEAT

Heat is very effective in killing bed bugs. The difficulty of treating with heat is reaching the killing temperature of 118°F and holding it there for at least one hour. Circulating the heat so that it penetrates every spot in the home is also a problem. Several well-placed fans will be needed. Most companies raise the heat slowly while reducing or holding the humidity stable throughout the process. This is important so that televisions, computers, and wood furniture don't get damaged. In most cases it will take four to six hours to reach the killing temperature, then an hour holding at the killing temperature, and then three to six hours to reduce the temperature again. The entire process may take eight to twelve total hours to do it right. Heat is used when an individual cannot or doesn't want to use chemical treatments. Perhaps they have small children and do not want them exposed to pesticides. It is the clients who choose and pay for the service—and it should be provided as they choose. However, I always warn my clients that there is no protection against reinfestation since there is no residual involved.

Heat treatments *do not* prevent reinfestations. Once the temperature reaches ambient levels bed bugs may re-occupy the home.

When bed bugs are exposed to 118°F their cells start to denature or fall apart. Adults and nymphs die within five minutes, although it may take up to thirty minutes. Eggs are much harder to kill and may take up to one hour to die. Higher temperatures, around 125–130°F, will kill in minutes.

A word of warning—do not use space heaters, barbecue, open fires, and other devices to kill bed bugs in your home. I saw someone on the news in Massachusetts who tried to use a barbeque to heat a bedroom and set the home on fire. I know anyone who has a bed bug infestation will be incredibly frustrated, but please be sensible.

CYRONITE

Freezing with cryonite using specialized equipment will kill bed bugs and the eggs on contact—it is an environmentally friendly option as it does not use chemicals. Because of this fact, some government agencies only permit the use of cyronite when treating their buildings. This method is also preferred by places where food is prepared because it is chemical free and does not require evacuation or closing of the premises while being administered. The technicians using cryonite must be trained to use this highly specialized equipment that is expensive to buy and maintain. Companies need to have several on hand as replacement parts can take several weeks to arrive from their manufacturer in Europe. Cryonite will also not penetrate as deeply as heat. Both heat and cryonite have no residual qualities and therefore bed bugs may reinfest the home immediately after treatment. This is a tool to be used in areas where insecticides and other treatment cannot be used or have failed.

Bed bugs are capable of tolerating temperatures, as low as 32°F for several days (Unsinger 1966).

Because of the high cost and limited penetration qualities of cryonite, steam should be an alternative in many cases.

If you are worried about televisions, computers, and other electronic equipment having bed bugs then short bursts of compressed air will allow you to find out if bed bugs are inside the equipment without the expense. These cans of compressed air may be found in the computer section of any store—we use them to clean keyboards and other surfaces. Be careful since they are designed to be used only in short bursts and only a few times. Always follow the directions on the label.

Cleanup and Follow-up

Every pest management treatment requires an inspection immediately—as soon as the job is completed. The technician is required to reinspect the areas treated for spillage, equipment that may be left behind, and to determine if the job was performed correctly. They should ideally take the time to go over the process with you, review the job, and answer any of your questions. If the client is satisfied, then they will sign the contract reflecting their complete satisfaction and payment rendered. Always remember your own needs and your peace of mind at this stage. If you are not satisfied do not sign until you are satisfied.

The problem with having this final review with your PMP is that bed bug work may require you to hang around for hours while they complete treatment. This may be impractical. The other hindrance is that you cannot enter the premises until the materials used in treatment are dry. If a medical condition exists, the client may have to wait until the next day to return. The elderly, young children, and individuals with breathing problems should be more cautious. This is usually explained on the preparation sheet provided prior to the job being scheduled—many clients take these sheets listing the chemicals we plan to use and consult with their doctor to be on the safe side. Remember, only the technician who performed the job can accurately inspect and review if the job was done right immediately after job completion.

As far as follow-ups are concerned, many pest management firms will return ten to twenty days later to reinspect the location. Different companies have different approaches, some will only reinspect while others will automatically re-treat. I don't like to re-treat unless it is needed—the less chemicals used overall, the better. Live bed bugs found during a follow-up inspection is cause for re-treatment. One reason live bed bugs may still be present is the areas not treated with residuals can still have bed bug eggs which will hatch ten to twenty-one days later. A client who is complaining of still being bitten *with no evidence of live bed bugs* is not cause for re-treatment. Remember, a fee may be incurred for the follow-up, separate from the initial cost of the job. The fee for the follow-up visit should be made clear on the contract prior to the initial job. It should be much lower than the cost of the initial visit. Companies may charge anywhere from $150 dollars to over a thousand, depending on the size and scope of the work involved. If the job cost a lot the first time, it will cost a lot the second time as well.

What Does It Mean to be "Green?"

Most customers want to reduce their overall exposure to pesticides. Many conscientious building owners are trying to qualify under new "green standards" which are set in order to reduce exposure to pesticides and other harsh chemicals in and around structures. To verify that a true standard is met, many pest management companies have hired an independent organization such as Green Shield. Green Shield has set the following basic standards for certifying pest management companies as "green":

- Use a prevention-based approach, applying effective nonchemical strategies first and pesticides only when necessary.

- Use approved methods of application when pesticides are needed, such as baits and traps.

- Use only pesticides that have been screened and approved by Green Shield Certified.

None of the pesticides used can carry a "warning or danger" label. They cannot be listed even as *possibly* carcinogenic on the EPA's or the California 65's list.

So when it comes to treating for bed bugs, this reduces the overall choices of pesticides and increases other aspects of integrated pest management methods such as sealing cracks and crevices, or sanitation. This includes using mattress encasements and increased use of monitoring devices.

Preparation by the customer remains about the same. Items such as books, electronics, artwork, and such will have to be placed in heat chambers, treated with steam, or treated with cryonite. Success will vary.

A bed bug client choosing a green method should expect more vacuuming, use of heat methods such as steam, and the use of diatomaceous earth instead of pyrethrin or pyrethoid dusts in wall voids. (Diatomaceous earth is a naturally occurring fine powder made of sedimentary rock, which acts to absorb lipids from the outer layer of a bed bug's exoskeleton—causing them to dehydrate and die after a few days.) Less residual products may be applied.

This type of treatment is difficult and more time consuming. Repeat treatments may be necessary to achieve good results. Overall pesticide use is reduced—and if that is important to you, then this will be a method to consider.

CHAPTER 5

CASE STUDIES

First Encounter

My first encounter with bed bugs came during a routine visit to a small walk-up apartment building in the Greenpoint section of Brooklyn, New York. On the first floor in a railroad style apartment, I met a gentleman from Eastern Europe. He indicated that he was being bitten and pointed to the small bed that was up against the wall in a greatly cluttered room. In broken English, he explained to me that he believed he had brought over from his country some bed bugs. I didn't believe him—remember, bed bugs were not common until just a few years ago. I was repulsed at the thought. I examined the area and did find some. I collected some live samples to take back to the company I was working for at the time. I then treated the area with the only product I had inside my compressed air sprayer—it must have been an organophosphate or carbamate, which is what we used back then. I never treated the mattress directly. I moved the bed away from the wall and treated the cracks and crevices around the bed. I told him to wash the linen repeatedly. I explained that I had to come back to provide follow-up treatment and asked him to take the bed apart for when I returned.

With tremendous patience, this gentleman awaited my arrival one month later. He followed my instructions and had the bed dismantled, which allowed me to treat the bed frame. I also re-treated the perimeter of the entire room.

On my third visit, this gentleman told me that he no longer had bed bugs. I was happy and he was happy.

What I learned was that I needed to overcome my own fear of bed bugs, and I was grateful that my first encounter with them was an easy one. I was amazed how patient and tolerant the gentleman was of the pest. He obviously had encountered them before and had learned to deal with them. I would later learn just how tolerant humans can be.

It was during this time in history that the Berlin Wall came down and the Eastern European countries began opening up to international travel and commerce. Bed bugs were about to explode into this country as a result.

Second Encounter

The second time I encountered bed bugs was in the Jackson Heights area of Queens County, New York. Queens is the most diverse borough, with over 140 different countries represented. Of the five boroughs, Queens also has the most trees. Jackson Heights has many prewar apartment buildings which surround interior courtyards. Within one of these apartments that consisted of approximately forty to sixty units in the early 1990s, I got a call to treat for cockroaches. At this time in my career, I was working for my own company.

A lovely young lady in her late twenties lived in a studio apartment. She requested monthly pest control service for cockroaches.

On this particular visit, she explained to me that she had been receiving bites at night on a regular basis for several weeks. Being late summer, I asked her if she kept her windows open at night or if she went for evening walks. She said that neither applied. I then asked a rare question. "Did you buy a used piece of furniture or pick something up used?" She said yes. "I picked up this used chair in the curbside trash."

Many individuals comb the trash for items that may be recycled, and furniture is one of the top items taken. This is actually illegal in the city of New York. Once an item is placed out for trash, then it becomes the property of the Department of Sanitation. They rarely issue a summons for such an act. At the time I had known some DSNY personnel to take furniture and bicycles to refurbish and resell. This practice is less common now.

I examined the chair and found evidence of bed bug fecal matter. I explained to her what the issue was. I had a product that was considered a wide spectrum insecticide in my compressed air sprayer which would take care of it. A wide spectrum insecticide covers many insects—the one I had included bed bugs on the label, so I knew it would do the trick. I treated the cracks and crevices along the bottom of the chair and around the perimeter of the bedroom, which had an open threshold to the living room where the chair was located.

About two weeks later, I received a call from her to please come by. She explained that although things had gotten better, she was starting to be bitten again. I then told her to have her apartment ready for my next treatment by removing her linens from the bed and vacuuming the entire apartment.

When I arrived, I saw that she had followed my instructions. She was a bit nervous and was worried that the materials I was using would cause her harm. I told her that once dried, the product would not harm her. I inspected around the bed and found evidence of bed bugs and live bed bugs in the joints of the bed frame.

This time, I attacked the cracks and crevices around the perimeter first. I had learned by doing this that I would prevent migration of the insects into adjoining areas, such as the next-door apartment. The organophosphates of the time had a relatively strong odor associated with them. Many customers of that time didn't believe the exterminator was spraying with something strong unless it had a foul odor.

I also brought with me an Actisol machine that I would use for deep penetration. This machine works like a large aerosol can. It is designed to push an insecticide deep into voids by using compressed air. I used it in the crevices on the hardwood floors. Her apartment had many small gaps and I was worried that the bed bugs would hide between the hardwood floor and the subflooring. I rarely used dust—one of the common treatments today—but in this case I used a pyrethrum dust common at the time. I asked her to vacate the apartment for several hours to allow the products to settle and dry.

On my next regular monthly visit, she was glad that the ordeal was finally over. She still had questions though. She asked, "Where do bed bugs come from and why did they hide in the furniture? I thought they stayed on the mattresses." I explained that the times were changing; new immigrants were moving into the neighborhood and were bringing the bed bugs with them. DDT hasn't been allowed to be used for many years. I also explained that the pest control industry was now moving away from routine baseboard perimeter spraying toward treating only the areas where insects hide and feed. Baits were now being used widely to attract cockroaches and ants to feed on the products and return to their "nest" and share the materials and die. Far less pesticides were being applied and more targeted applications were being done.

Reviewing this encounter, I realized that I could not put my compressed air sprayer away—it would remain a valuable tool regardless of the success of the modern baits for cockroaches and ants. As a matter of fact, I still have the same one with me. I will not let it go.

I would not have to deal with bed bugs again until 2001. Travel and new markets opened up in Europe, Asia,

Africa, and South America. New immigrants moved into our country at astonishing rates. New York City grew to over eight million people by the 2000 census.

Remember, at the turn of this century very few individuals were studying bed bugs. One individual that has maintained a strain of bed bugs for study since World War II is Dr. Harold J Harlan. I have met him several times throughout the years at seminars sponsored by our regional and national pest management associations. He is a very nice man and willing to impart knowledge to anyone who wishes to listen. I believe it was during a visit to Purdue University's annual pest management conference that Dr. Harlan spoke about the effects of Gentrol IGR on cockroaches. He also mentioned the product may have some chitin-inhibiting qualities (chitin is the main component in the exoskeleton of insects). Gentrol IGR is an insect growth regulator that mimics the juvenile hormone found inside of insects. As long as the hormone is present, the insect cannot reach maturity or reproduce. It sterilizes the eggs while the female carries them. This way the egg may be laid but will remain non-viable. Adults don't die from it—they just become sterile. But that aspect wasn't what interested me at the time. I had been dealing with a termite baiting system that was a chitin inhibitor. It disrupted the ability of the termites to complete the molting process. Knowing that bed bugs molt after each blood meal, I thought it may help in breaking their life cycle. Used with another adulticide, it could end bed bug infestations more quickly.

Dr. Harlan happened to have brought some of his bed bugs in a jar and while we were talking a colleague, Patrick

Corallo, placed the open jar on his arm to feed them. We wondered if, because Gentrol had chitin inhibiting qualities, it might also be useful against bed bugs. Dr. Harlan soon after received a grant to study the effects of Gentrol IGR on bed bugs. Within a little over a year, the product received an additional labeling for use against bed bugs.

I started to incorporate Gentrol along with several other products on any new bed bug jobs I performed.

A footnote to the meeting we had with Dr. Harlan. Several days later, Pat developed a circular rash on his forearm. He said to me, "Ralph I was taking a shower when I noticed this rash, but I don't know what it's from?" I said, "Pat, don't you remember, that's the spot you put the jar of bed bugs on." It was a perfect circle—and yet he hadn't felt any of the bed bugs bite.

As we continue with these stories, you will see that not everyone reacts to bed bugs in the same way. Pat's rash lasted well over a week.

Third Encounter

My third encounter took place in and around 2002. Both Pat Corallo and I serviced this client in Long Island City, Queens. By this time, we were becoming aware that bed bugs were on the rise. We never met the tenant since they had left for work. The superintendant let us in. Both Pat and I had asked the client to prepare for treatment by laundering their clothing. We asked that the linen on the bed not be moved so as to let us find the bed bugs and eliminate them. We spent a minimum of four hours in this apartment. It was a one bedroom. We vacuumed everything, the bed, baseboards, furniture, etc. We used a product called Suspend SC, a liquid suspended concentrate, according to the label. It was the only product that had a residual, which allowed us to treat both the mattress and furniture at the same time. We also used Gentrol IGR since it now had the label for bed bug use. In New York State, we need to have the pest approved for treatment on the label before it can be used. It was tedious.

This apartment had several pockets of bed bugs. Most were found along the bed frame. We had to use a screwdriver to disassemble the captain's bed, also known as a platform bed with drawers under it.

It was in the corners of this platform bed that most of the bed bugs would hide. We found eggs, nymphs, and adults. Other areas that contained bed bugs were behind the floorboards or baseboard moldings. Several bed bugs would emerge once the treatment was performed.

Since we were so thorough in performing this job, we both felt confident that a follow-up treatment would not be necessary. As it turned out, it wasn't.

The lessons I learned during this job were how important it is to inspect carefully, have the client be prepared, be able to work with the client while they were *out* of our work zone, and to have the time to treat properly. All of these factors existed on this job and allowed us the comfort of knowing that an excellent job was done.

Fourth Case Study

Within a year, everything was changing. The company I was working for was in transition from a small family business to a medium-sized company with individuals receiving job titles and specific duties. I was still in the field but trying to convince the owners that I should have a manager's position while continuing to work in the field. Hal Byer, the owner of Magic Exterminators, has been in the pest control business since 1960. He understood that for his company to reach the next level of service, professional individuals would need to take control and lead the company in a new direction. New technicians meant lots of training. It would take two full years before the technicians would be experienced enough to treat without assistance or guidance. Now the team is strong and experienced.

It was during this time that I had to service an account in Nassau County that consisted of garden-style apartments. There were two apartments per entry with one apartment above the other. In this case, the second floor apartment complained of getting bitten, but our inspection of the unit revealed a very clean apartment with very few items in it. We told management that we needed to inspect the ground-floor apartment.

Our inspection of the ground-floor apartment revealed a very serious infestation. The two-bedroom apartment had a queen-size bed in the master bedroom with an additional bunk bed setup. So in the master bedroom alone there were at least four individuals sleeping. The

This is the wall in the children's bedroom.

second bedroom had only one queen-size bed, but after interviewing the tenant I found out that four additional children slept there.

When I first entered the room, I thought I was looking at wallpaper with designs on it. Upon closer inspection, I found myself looking at squashed bed bugs or blood smears all over the wall. The children spent most of their time at night killing bed bugs by smashing them on the walls. I couldn't believe my eyes. It stopped me dead in my tracks. I thought I would be performing a casual inspection. Now I knew I had to look very closely at everything.

I found out that they had picked up used mattresses from the garbage, which is likely how the infestation began.

I tried very hard to explain what they needed to do to get prepared for our treatment.

Within three days, we returned for the treatment. They tried their best to prepare. It wasn't good enough. They hadn't removed anything from the floors, and all of the bagged items were left on the bed. They didn't remove all the clothing from the closets. At this time, we didn't have a policy of walking away when someone wasn't ready. We just treated the best we could. The other problem was a warranty. We gave them one. What a mistake that was.

When a pest control company goes into an apartment such as this to treat for bed bugs, the technician tries to set up a safe zone. This helps in moving items around the room. There was a team of six technicians on this project. In this one building, we had both apartments to service: one team upstairs and one downstairs. One was an easy job to perform and the other a nightmare. Bed bugs were found everywhere in the first floor apartment. I would find out during treatment that this family was using the living room as a bedroom as well—that came to a total of ten individuals living in a two bedroom apartment. *Wow!* I felt very bad for them and the clients upstairs.

What we didn't know at this time was that one of the products we were using, Suspend SC, was no longer as effective against bed bugs. Resistance was developing. As each generation of bed bugs is born, they carry with them the genetic information from their parents. If we expose one hundred bed bugs to a product and kill 95 percent of them, those are pretty good odds. The five that are left will breed the next generation with more resistance so now you have 10 percent to 20 percent alive. The next generation after that may have up to 25 percent survivors. This continues until as long as the same product or family of products is used. The problem is that until recently, the pest management industry has had primarily only one family of product available to use against bed bugs, the pyrethroids. It is now known according to a study by Dr. Michael Potter of the University of Kentucky, that a strain of bed bugs we supplied him from New York City, Far Rockaway region, is resistant up to three hundred times the label rate of Suspend SC.

We had to return to this location several times over the next thirty days to fulfill our contract and to control this infestation. We would have to perform many treatments over the next several months before the management would find it too expensive to continue working with us.

I don't know if they ever got complete eradication of the bed bug infestation at this location. We as a pest management company learned to change our preparation procedures and treatment procedures due to our experience with this account.

Again, the level of tolerance those individuals had amazes me. The clutter and level of infestation that would drive many of us mad or insane is just plain normal to many other individuals. When individuals accept that somehow it is OK to live under these conditions, that is going to allow bed bugs to escalate over the next several years as the infestations get worse.

Fifth Case Study

This next case is fascinating because of how it got started. Our sister company, Suburban Pest Management LLC, is run by Hal's brother Marty. He also is in the process of passing on his part of the business to his children. In charge of the day-to-day operations are the general manager, Robert Wiemer, and the technical director, Lynn Frank. Mr. Wiemer received a call from this client to investigate a complaint of bed bugs at his Far Rockaway apartment complex. This location consisted of three-story buildings with two hallways of approximately ten apartments running down each one. Mr. Wiemer spoke with the tenant and was shocked to see live bed bugs crawling on the individual. As we sometimes do to aid further research and study of bed bugs, we decided that we would collect live samples from this location prior to treatment—Dr. Michael of the University of Kentucky and several other individuals had requested live specimens from the field.

We videotaped our inspection and collection. There were four of us, Robert Wiemer, Lynn Frank, Patrick Corallo, and I. We wore disposable Tyvek suits with hoods. I was the last one in the apartment, and I wasn't wearing my hood.

It was an average-sized one-bedroom apartment. When you entered, the kitchen was on your left and the living room straight ahead. A small hallway with a closet led to the bathroom and the one bedroom. There was a popcorn ceiling.

Within five steps, I noticed a nymph on my chest. I told Pat that I had on my Tyvek suit. I had not touched anything. His cursing can be heard on the video tape. The bed bugs were in the popcorn ceiling and falling on us. They were protected, I was not. I probably had them in my hair. I stayed until the collection was done. We had *heard* stories of this happening, yet here we were—two board-certified entomologist experiencing it firsthand. I noticed that only the nymphs were willing to fall from the ceiling onto us. It happened several times during the collection process. I continued collecting the bed bugs with them. We must have collected hundreds of live bed bugs. They were everywhere. They were in the dentures, toothbrush, dressers, ceiling, walls, baseboards, sofa, dining room table, inside groceries, and in a picture frame of the last supper. When these bed bugs were tested by Dr. Potter, it was found that they were resistant to Suspend SC. Not just that, they were resistant to three hundred times the label rate of Suspend SC. They would also be resistant to the product Tempo WP or SC.

Other tenants on the floor had powder in front of their doors in hope of preventing the bed bugs from entering their apartments.

Back in this unit, the bed bugs would end up being difficult to kill off. At this point, we didn't know that these bed bugs had developed such a strong resistance to the

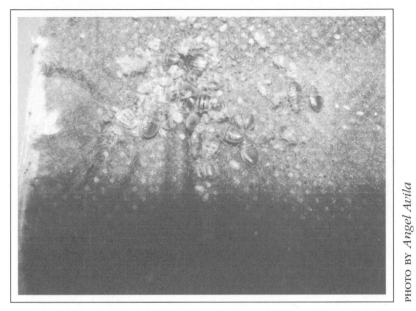

PHOTO BY *Angel Avila*

Cluster of bed bugs under the couch

Bed bugs along the ceiling and wall junction

PHOTO BY *Angel Avila*

PHOTO BY *Angel Avila*

A bed bug reacting to chemical treatment

Bed bugs under the lining of the box spring mattress

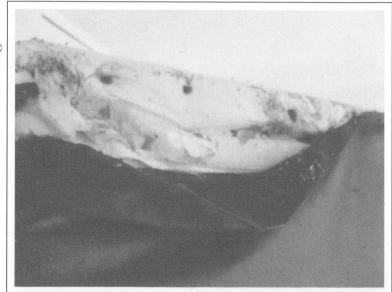

PHOTO BY *Angel Avila*

commonly used products. The products that the other tenants were buying were being used in their apartments without following the label directions, which called for them to be mixed with a gallon of water. Their mentality was the stronger the better. The health consequences don't matter to an individual who purchases products like this. They just want results. This is the same as dropping a nuclear bomb to kill off a few individuals. I don't know if this behavior affected the speed with which bed bugs became resistant, but it didn't help the industry.

We had to cooperate with a government agency to help the individual who lived in this apartment. This person was ill mentally. This person didn't even realize that they were getting bitten. Everyone else around them did. By the time it became evident that this individual was the centralized cause of the infestation, most of the building had bed bugs. It would cost several thousand dollars and many months of treatments and re-treatment until the infestation would come under control. Even today we still have to go back every few months and treat some of the units in this location. Reinfestation occurs rapidly in places where the tenants don't have the money to launder their clothing and bedding. Often tenants are under the belief that this is management's problem alone. In the earlier case that took place in Long Island City, the landlord paid for entirely new content of the apartment. It must have cost him thousands of dollars. Often landlords are of the belief that it is a tenant's problem and that they shouldn't have to get involved. Many of the health codes and new laws force them to resolve any pest problems within a rental or cooperative building.

Dealing with mentally ill individuals requires providing assistance to them during every step of the process. It is important to help them understand that they don't need to live under these conditions. Trust is very important during this process. If at any time the individual loses trust in the process, you may never get rid of the infestation. They need the support of a loved one. We do our best to provide support as well. Once the job is done, compassion doesn't end. Reinspect the unit and help them understand the possibility that reinfestation may reoccur if they are not more careful. This applies to every bed bug client that Pest Management Professionals encounter. From the preparation, inspection, treatment, and reinspection, a PMP must be knowledgeable, thoughtful, patient, and understanding.

Sixth Case Study

In a wealthier part of Nassau County, a detached one-family house presented a case were the wife and three lovely children were complaining of being bitten. Inspecting the house was time consuming. It took several hours. Starting in the son's room, I found nothing. There are no blood marks, nothing. No sign of any bed bugs. In the daughter's room, I found blood droppings, yet no live bed bugs. I was getting frustrated. Where is the source of this infestation? And how could the children and the wife be bitten and not the husband? The master bedroom was very large. I inspected the king-size bed, moving the linen aside, examining the corners. Astonished, I realized that the husband was getting bitten all along. Most of the bed bugs were on his side of the bed. Everything made sense after interviewing the wife. She explained to me that her husband constantly traveled for business. He must have brought them into the house. He told me that he felt nothing. No bites. I explained to him that some individuals don't react to the bed bug bite. This is also true for some individuals who get bitten by mosquitoes. He seemed to understand, especially when I showed him the bed bugs on his side of the bed. The reason the children would get bitten was because they all joined the parents on the bed to watch television at night. This is when the bed bugs would quietly feed on the children.

Preparation was extensive since this family had lots of stuffed animals and luggage. Laundering took days. It took them a better part of a week to prepare. Vacuuming every room took time as well. The treatment was easy—it just took all day. I was more worried about staining the dark wood molding throughout the house. Some of our products leave small white droplets that appear to stain. One of our products today contains isopropyl alcohol, which if you are not careful may damage the glossy finish on some furniture.

I reminded the husband that care needs to be taken when traveling. Bed bugs may be picked up at the airport when the luggage is stored with other luggage. It may occur in the hotel. It may occur on the return trip. Constant inspection of your luggage, carry-on bags, and you body is vital to ensure that bed bugs are not brought into the home. I cannot say this enough. Early detection is crucial. Wash all your clothing as soon as you return home, including the clothes you're wearing. Inspect the luggage for signs of bed bugs. Create a safe zone in the garage or entry to your place of residence.

Seventh Case Study

In another typical Cape Cod home in Nassau County, I inspected for bed bugs. This client was very specific as to where the bed bugs were located. They insisted that the bed bugs were only found upstairs in the master bedroom. Inspecting this room, I found one specimen.

In my interview with the client, I found out that they didn't travel and had no one visit. They didn't understand why they would have bed bugs, nor did I. The Cape Cods are designed with a second floor which would be the attic on most homes. In this case it was converted into bedrooms. In order to deal with the slope of the roofline, small walls that form closets or knee walls are designed. That was the case here. This house was located at the end of a dead-end street with a forested area beyond.

I thought about this long and hard. I brought the specimen back to my home and placed it under my microscope. I noticed the long hair behind the eye. After referring to my textbook, I realized that I had a bat bug. Bat bugs are very similar to bed bugs, except that they have longer hairs. I reported this back to the client who revealed to me that years earlier, they did have bats in the knee walls.

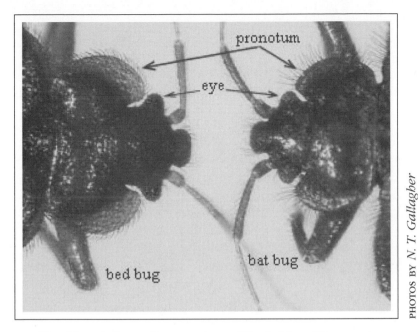

The fringe hairs on the pronotum of the bat bug (R) are as long as or longer than the width of the eye, whereas these hairs are shorter in the bed bug (L).

In combination with a wildlife expert, we timed our treatment. In this case that stopped the infestation and the client was happy. If another, less experienced Pest Management Professional treated this client without excluding the bats, the infestation would have continued. "Excluding the bats" is done by waiting for them to leave in the evening and then sealing the opening they used to leave. Sometimes we have to look at both the indoor and outdoor environment to find the solution. This is often forgotten by PMP's in an urban environment. Where bats are more common, this may occur more often.

Eighth Case Study

In midtown Manhattan, one of our service managers, James Tallman, or Jimmy to his friends, inspected a small walk-up apartment building. This building was attached on both sides and was in the middle of the block. This area is in the theater district of New York, where many tenants work on Broadway. This building had two apartments on the first floor and four apartments on each of the next four floors. They are designed as railroad apartments consisting of either a studio or one-bedroom units. In this particular building, many of the tenants tried to take care of the bed bug infestation on their own. When they couldn't solve the problem, they complained to the owners. The owners were lovely individuals who have owned the building for a very long time and wanted a solution.

Jimmy came to me for help writing the proposal. It was one of the more detailed proposals we have written. This was a time when we always wrote our proposals with a thirty- or sixty-day warranty. With a warranty, we would go back at our cost every time the customer called to complain. What we found was that many times the customer didn't launder or prepare properly, which led to reinfestation. Thus it would cost us time and money since they didn't take the preparation seriously. Preparation is at least half of the work. Reinfestation can and will happen very easily. No one had a code of practice in place. We were all learning by experience. This proposal would be different. The job would consist of treating all eighteen units in the building. The price tag would be over $9,000. I made sure we modified the contract to call for reduced prices on any follow-up inspection or treatment. This assured us of not losing money if we had to return at any time.

We completed the service and realized that it must have started in one third-floor unit in which an older gentleman lived. He kept an illegal roommate at the time who had just arrived from another country a few months earlier, and whom we suspected of bringing in the bed bugs. Compounding the issue was the fact that the older gentleman, although surely being bitten, didn't have a reaction to the bites.

When his roommate complained of recurring bites a few months later, this older gentleman refused a repeated service. We decided to start drilling into the wall voids, including the ceilings, to try to prevent the bed bugs from moving throughout the building. It seemed to reduce the problem for a time.

Several months later, more tenants complained and decided to withhold their rent. This forced the owners to start legal proceedings against the older gentleman. Without his cooperation, elimination of the infestation wasn't going to happen. I helped the owners by providing written documents of the service visits performed and the frequency of refusal by this individual. Believe me—I don't like doing this. A city agency got involved to assist this person to cooperate. This took time, and the bed bug infestation got worse. Months later, the courts assisted this gentleman in cooperating. He didn't prepare, but we tried the best we could. This led to more court hearings, and in time he moved out. The entire process took over one and a half years. It took another six months to get control of the bed bugs after he left.

When it becomes necessary to involve government or various agencies along with tenants, owners, property managers, and staff, bed bug control becomes a daunting task. No other insect or pest has made the process of cooperation and treatment so difficult. This is true throughout history, as some of the previous chapters have shown.

What was lacking in this one case was education. The tenants and ownership didn't know the pest. The local government was totally unprepared to handle these cases. There were too many questions and myths out there. We weren't quite ready either. We thought that we could just tell them to prepare, and we would take care of the pest. The clients really needed to understand the habits and biology so that they could inform us what was happening. This mutual understanding also serves to reduce the tension and confusion when the miracle elimination of the bed bugs doesn't occur after the first treatment.

Our lessons learned from this case study for future jobs include going into the building prior to treatment with a powerpoint presentation for the staff, property managers, and tenants. We presented the basic knowledge of identification, biology, habitat, and treatment of the bed bug. This would still create questions, but most would be answered prior to treatment. We have found that most clients are better prepared with fewer re-treatments required.

Ninth Case Study

In Brooklyn, I met with a woman in an apartment building on the first floor. My office called me to swing by and inspect this apartment–she was complaining about fleas. It was flea season in New York, which takes place from mid to late summer. The problem was that this person claimed that the fleas were localized under her bathroom sink. I suspected she didn't have fleas. I suspected what she had was a case of delusions of parasitosis. This is a form of psychosis where a person has false belief that insects are infesting their home or body. When I arrived, she wanted me to wear a Tyvek suit. I declined to wear one. She was aghast that I entered her apartment with no protection and inspected under her sink. I found nothing. I then sat down with her and went over her story. She thought she had brought sand fleas back from Puerto Rico in the winter and she thought she still had them. She had already been treated by another company and wanted us to take care of it because the other company didn't resolve her problem. I told her there was nothing we could do other than place out monitors or plain glue boards to see if something would turn up. She started to cry. Sometimes we just cannot help people. We need to know our limitations.

In another bed bug case where I suspected delusions of parasitosis, the client lived in an apartment building in Queens. Our inspector found one bed bug in her apartment and showed it to the management. The tenant began calling our office multiple times a day. This went on for more than a week. Our technicians found nothing further during the treatment. She even insisted that her car be treated. She claimed she was continuously being bitten. Customer service transferred her calls to me. I answered all her questions calmly even when they got outrageous. She thought she was seeing bed bugs crawling on her vacuum cleaner. I told her that I would see her the next morning. She called back several times. I explained to her that I had work to do and needed her to calm down and wait until morning. I felt bad, but I had to be firm.

The next morning, I inspected her apartment. Aside from cigarette ashes and some dust, she had nothing. If she did have bed bugs, it was a very low infestation. So what was biting her? She insisted that every little piece of lint, ash, dust, or other particles that she had me inspect was a bed bug. I inspected some of the specimens under a microscope. I thought maybe her cat was suffering a very specific mite called *Cheyletiella*, which causes very intense itching. So I recommended that the cat see a vet and that she see a dermatologist. She agreed.

She called back the next day. I explained to her that I would not take any more calls until she saw both a vet and a dermatologist. Several days later she called back to tell me that no fleas or mites were found on the cat. So again I explained to her that she still needed to see the dermatologist.

Days later she called again. The doctor placed her on scabies medication. I had forgotten all about scabies. How she got it I don't know. Treatment was now being rendered.

Days later she called again. She reported no longer being bitten. What a relief.

We all need to realize that other pests do bite. This pest must be included in our inspection, and we shouldn't fool ourselves into believing that all bites are due to bed bugs. Fleas bite, lice bite, bird mites bite, and mosquitoes bite. So if you don't find the bed bug or any evidence of bed bugs—don't assume bed bugs. Don't *insist* that they are bed bugs. We need to inspect, prepare, and be sensible. This is for our own mental and physical health.

Tenth Case Study

This case study happened while writing this book. The client had a single-family house in Brooklyn. This client was a ninety-year-old man. Although his entire house needed to be treated, he only wanted two rooms done. The initial inspector described it as "a crime scene." He told me that there was blood everywhere in the bedroom. The sheets, ruffles, pillowcases, everything had blood. The bed bugs were crawling everywhere. He wrote the contract outside. I asked him why we weren't going to treat the entire house. He said the man didn't want to as it was going to be too expensive. I called one of our field supervisors and asked if he would mind taking pictures. He called me awhile later and told me, "I'm scared." The bed bugs were crawling everywhere. He was afraid of taking them home.

I spoke with this field supervisor and the technician on the job after they finished. This individual couldn't prepare. The bed bugs were in the hallway. Both technicians

Blood and dropping on the mattress

Blood stains all over the pillow

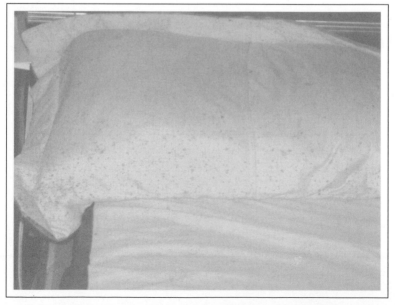

Skin casings of the bed bugs after they molt
as well as live bed bugs

told me that they had never seen anything like this, including the Far Rockaway building with the bugs dropping from the popcorn ceiling. As the gentleman was leaving so that the treatment could commence, our technician took a picture of the gentleman's shirt.

The problem often begins with family in this type of case. Did this older man have family that could help? If so, why weren't they aware of the situation? If he didn't have family, who do we call to assist this man who obviously cannot help himself? Maybe he doesn't want the help? How do we convince him? Does our government have the power to force him into controlling this problem? What is the process? These are the many questions that need an answer. We probably will not agree with all of them, but we do need to know.

These are live bed bugs on the client's shirt:

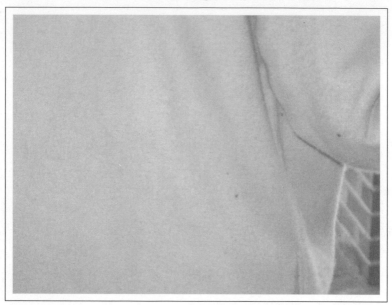

More live bed bugs on the client's shirt:

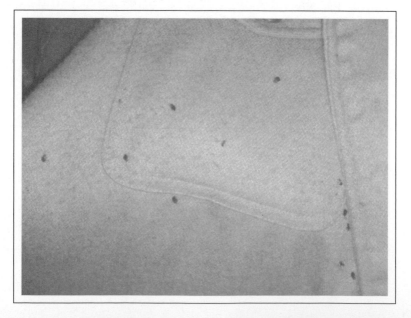

CHAPTER 6

WHAT THE NEAR AND DISTANT FUTURE HOLDS

Government and Laws

Government is at its best when giving guidance and direction. The following article demonstrates what happens when good government can help solve these problems:

BE CAREFUL FIGHTING BED BUGS, FLORIDA OFFICIALS SAY.

WITH INFESTATIONS UP, CONSUMERS MAY RISK INJURY FROM PESTICIDES

People and their pets have been hurt when they misused pesticides and chemical bombs trying to combat pesky bed bugs that are making a comeback in the nation's hotels, institutions and bed-rooms, Florida officials said Tuesday.

"People get desperate when they are trying to treat these bugs by themselves because they are such a tenacious pest and they are so adept at hiding themselves," said Michael Page, a spokes-man for the Florida Department of Agriculture and Consumer Affairs.

Florida has not become a hotbed for bed bugs so far, but officials said complaints and problems are steadily rising. So far this year, Florida hotels have been cited for 81 infestations – including 11 in *Broward County* and four in *Palm Beach County* as recently as last month.

All the cited hotels wiped out their outbreaks with professional extermination, but a few have had repeat visits from the biters, state figures show. No one tracks outbreaks in other settings, but exterminators have reported increased calls from homeowners and other businesses.

The little pests are not known to carry diseases, but they can greatly annoy their victims with fero-cious and repeated biting.

In other states where bed bugs are more wide-spread, frustrated consumers have tried arming themselves with pesticides, chemicals such as al-cohol and store-bought bug bombs. But the result too often has been failure to eliminate bed bug outbreaks, causing repeat infestations, Page said. Also, pesticides applied improperly can cause burns or rashes on people and pets. In a few cases, families using multiple bug bombs—which don't work against bed bugs—have caused small explosions.

"We don't know of anything like that in Florida. But it's something we're concerned about and trying to avoid by educating the public," said David Krause, a toxicologist at the Florida Department of Health.

State officials give these tips in the battle against bed bugs:

Inspect items after traveling before bringing them into the home. Take all precautions to keep bed bugs out. Travel is a main way they spread from place to place.

Look for dark bugs the size of an apple seed, usually found in the seams of beds and sofas, behind headboards and elsewhere in the bedroom, backpacks and the like.

Signs of bed bugs include small brownish-red to purple spots on infested items.

Reduce clutter in your home to eliminate their hiding places.

Choose a licensed pest control company with experience managing bed bugs. Home treatments often do not succeed.

A single fumigation by a professional often does the trick. But repeat treatments may be needed, so be prepared to pay for it.

If self-treating, follow label guidelines for the use of any registered pesticide.

Bed bug monitors and traps are relatively inexpensive ways to find infestations. One possible source of information: http://bedbugger.com/forum/topic/homemade-bed-barriers-climbup-interceptors.

Bob LaMendola, *Sun Sentinel*,
November 9, 2010

Reprinted with permission from the *Sun Sentinel*.

In an article from the *New York Daily News,* columnist Lukas Alpert wrote that the US Congress met with Pest Management Professionals and victims of bed bug infestation in Washington to discuss a coordinated plan of attack. The writer states that the meeting grew out of the legislation that was passed the year before which provides $50 million for bed bug abatement programs throughout the country.

The federal government should continue to provide money for the leading experts to perform seminars across the country to educate citizens on how to identify, prepare, and find a Pest Management Professional for treatment. The guidance the federal level should provide is to the state governments in passing local legislation to allow for inspection in hotels, multiple dwellings, and commercial establishments. These hot spots may require periodic inspections to determine levels of infestation. The federal government should also provide monies for research and development of new chemistries and studies to combat bed bugs.

The state governments should be involved at the local level. Protection of our children in schools is priority number one. Find ways to help and protect our elderly. Provide agencies with the ability to assist individuals who cannot help themselves in arranging, preparing, and having the treatment done. Any medical care or the assistance in obtaining the care needed should be at the state or local level. Little steps with the assistance of the leading experts in the field to write and educate the general public are a good first step. Several forums have been or are being held near Washington, in Denver, and many other places throughout the United States.

Community Involvement

In New York City, a local community board led by the mayor's office, council people, city agencies, private health care providers, and other individuals are developing channels of communication to respond to complaints of bed bug infestation. We as a society must help those that cannot help themselves. NYC has a phone number (311) dedicated to handling these complaints. When someone calls, the phone operator takes the information down and contacts the appropriate department that needs to respond to the problem. *Sanitation will pick up any infested furniture and mattresses.* Now in NYC it is required by a new law enacted by the city council to bag the mattresses for disposal. This program began as of December 1, 2010. In public housing the NYC department of health and mental hygiene will dispatch inspectors and Pest Management Professional to help prepare apartments for treatment. Other examples of mobilization and cooperation are starting to take place in different forms throughout this country.

It is our responsibility as citizens to help the process of inspection, preparation, and treatments take place. In the middle of winter, many individuals check up on the elderly to make sure that they have heat and food. During these visits, we should be conscious of the conditions within the home to determine if bed bugs are present. If so, help the individual understand the importance of combating the problem before it gets worse. Perhaps it might require a little physical labor on our part to help prepare the home for treatment that the individual needs. Maybe we can help them find out who to contact for advice. Perhaps you will need to get a government agency involved. Most importantly, make sure the individual is comfortable with the approach being taken. The process is overwhelming. Do not abandon them at any time before, during, or after the process. They will need a friend, and you must be that person.

Everything starts with education—once you've educated yourself (not from hysterical websites but from legitimate resources) you can help educate others. *Don't rely on the "do-it-yourself" websites—it won't work.* You may suppress the problem for a while and drive them deeper into wall voids or into other apartments.

Research and Development

As I write this book, I am attending the Entomological Society of America's annual meeting in San Diego. During this meeting, there will be no less than nineteen different papers from university students and professors studying bed bugs. Some of the topics include the resistance of different products on bed bugs, understanding bed bug populations, using fungi to control bed bugs, using heat or cold, how bed bugs process adenosine triphosphate (ATP) for energy, and molecular research on bed bugs. Any one of these research methods may lead to a future breakthrough in bed bug control or elimination. This is how it starts: two years ago in the annual meeting pheromone research led to the development of several monitoring devices in use today. Although the pheromone combination is still under development, the use of the passive monitoring devices such as the CO_2-in-a-thermos is in standard use.

The major chemical companies are quietly looking at their inventory of agricultural products to see if any may be used in the pest management field to control bed bugs.

That will also take two to five years before we see it in the market place. New molecules designed specifically for destroying bed bugs are not known to be in development at this time since that costs far too much money. Only when these same chemical companies see a great potential for profit will they invest in the research necessary to develop a new molecule.

So for now we must be content with using a combination of different products and mechanical, physical, educational, and cooperative measures to combat the little vampires.

CHAPTER 7

104 THINGS TO KNOW ABOUT BED BUGS

Paul J. Bello is a pest management consultant. He provided me with permission to reprint this article from *Pest Management Professional*, a trade magazine. It is a very good question-and-answer instructional guide.

As an independent pest management consultant, over the recent past I've been involved with numerous bed bug situations, and received many calls and e-mails regarding bed bugs. In fact, bed bugs seem to take up a majority of my time. Since I do not advertise to the general public I'm usually surprised and impressed with the efforts non-industry folks take to find me. This past month I was contacted by a college student who is experiencing bed bugs in his apartment. That he took the time to search the net underscored his need for help.

Like many of you, in the field I've witnessed the desperation and suffering that folks have endured as a result of bed bugs. These folks are looking for information, answers to their concerns, and help to rid them of their bed bug problems. In response to this student's questions this list of 102 practical and useful things to know about bed bugs was written for your review. Please note that these bits of information were learned from first-hand field experience in dealing with bed bugs and working with industry colleagues across the country.

1. **Do not underestimate them: bed bugs take a lot of knowledge, experience, and time and effort to get rid of.**

2. You need to keep a heightened level of vigilance to be sure you never get bed bugs again.

3. **Bed bugs are "hitch-hikers" and largely dependent upon man to travel from place to place, so it's possible for you to bring bed bugs to other locations.**

4. It is possible for people to get bitten without knowing it.

5. **It is not necessary for bed bugs to feed every day or every week. They can "lay in wait" for the next host for surprisingly long periods of time.**

6. Bed bugs can last a long time without feeding. Some references indicate bed bugs can survive about one

year without feeding. Of course we are dealing with live entities and longevity is based upon local conditions. As such, your mileage may vary.

7. Until you have not seen a bed bug or have not been bitten for several weeks, some practitioners say as many as eight weeks, it may be wise to assume you still have bed bugs and act accordingly.

8. Bed bugs cannot climb smooth surfaces, such as clean glass or smooth plastic. Use this to your advantage and at least isolate your bed and furniture from bed bugs by using products such as the Insect Interceptor Climbup or glass jars that prevent bed bugs from being able to climb up your bed or furniture to bite you as you sleep.

9. Use suitable high quality mattress encasements or covers such as those by Protect-A-Bed or Mattress Safe to seal bed bugs in and take away the multiple hiding places on your mattress and box spring.

10. Some experts point out that, if necessary, bed bugs can get a blood meal from other bed bugs. While this may be a rare occurrence, it is possible and it underscores the tenacity of this troublesome pest.

11. Generally speaking, bed bugs can survive cold temperatures very well but succumb to heat rather easily. Recent industry literature cites temperatures of as low as about 113 degrees Fahrenheit for about 30 minutes

as being sufficient to kill bed bugs. Industry references and publications indicate a variety of temperatures and duration times to achieve mortality. It is likely best to be conservative to assure you achieve the desired results.

12. While live immature bed bugs and adults may be difficult to find, look for the "signs of bed bugs" including: fecal stains, eggs, and shed skins.

13. Much like mosquitoes, bed bugs suck blood from their host victims. These blood meals are sucked in through the piercing sucking mouthparts at the "north end" and later on are expelled out the south end as a dark ink-like-appearing fecal liquid. This fecal liquid creates the stains that may be found in areas where bed bugs travel and hide.

14. Bed bug eggs are tiny. They are about one millimeter long, that's only about $\frac{1}{32}$ of an inch.

15. Female bed bugs glue their eggs to hidden areas which can make it difficult to find and difficult to remove 100 percent of them using a vacuum.

16. Bed bug eggs are cylindrical and oval like, rounded at one end with a round flat hatch shape at the opposite end. The round flat end opens like a "round hatch top" when the immature bed bug emerges.

17.   Bed bug eggs are shiny, translucent, and a milky white color. After taking a blood meal immature bed bugs will turn dark and reddish brown. However, just like your mileage, color may vary.

18.   Hatched bed bug eggs appear hollow and may have their hatch top opened and attached or missing.

19.   Just like the eggs, newly emerged/hatched immature bed bugs are equally small and difficult to see.

20.   Newly hatched bed bugs are translucent, shiny, and milky white in color, making them difficult to see on light-colored mattresses and bedding materials.

21.   Bed bug eggs can be about the same size as one stitch of sewn mattress fabric.

22.   A simple $1.99 plastic magnifying glass found at an office supply store, K-Mart, Target, or Wal-Mart will make you a better bed bug finder. Of course, the better the lens quality, the better you will be able to see.

23.   You need a very good flashlight to optimize your hunt for bed bugs.

24.   An LED-type flashlight will serve you better than a normal bulb flashlight.

25. Reportedly alcohol, such as rubbing alcohol, kills bed bugs on contact.

26. At the time of this writing there are no university-research-proven bed bug repellent products currently available.

27. There are no effective university-research-proven "sonic electronic" repelling devices to rid your dwelling of bed bugs available at the time of this writing. However, this doesn't prevent the public from buying a surprising number of these sonic pest repelling devices each year.

28. Bed bug eggs hatch in about three to five days.

29. Generally speaking, bed bugs spend most of their time hiding.

30. Bed bugs prefer to hide in undisturbed areas.

31. In a home or apartment, the top hiding places for bed bugs seem to be the mattress, box spring, and bed frame.

32. In a hotel room, the top hiding place seems to be the headboard area.

33. When viewed from the side, bed bugs are built rather flat and adult bed bugs can be thinner than the thickness of a normal business card.

34. It's not always true that bed bugs "bite in a line" or "along a vein." It's likely that bed bug bites may appear to be in a line because of where the bed bug or bed bugs were located when they bit the victim, such as along the area where the victim's body was laying on the bed.

35. It seems that bed bugs do not bite where the body is covered by clothing or pajamas. However, it is possible for bed bugs to crawl underneath loose-fitting garments.

36. Adult bed bugs are about ¼ of an inch long by about ³⁄₁₆ inch wide.

37. As a snake does, bed bugs must molt or shed their skin to grow to the next stage of development (instar) until they become adults. These shed skins can be a telltale sign of the presence of bed bugs.

38. Bed bugs must have a blood meal to molt or grow to the next instar or stage of development.

39. Bed bugs go through five instars to become adults. This means an adult bed bug in your house may have fed upon you at least five times.

40.   There are no "albino bed bugs" (nor are there albino cockroaches). Bed bugs may appear light in color after molting and get their dark rusty red color after feeding.

41.   A bed bug's abdomen (the hind end area) grows many times its original size as it takes in your blood. Just check out one of the popular bed bug feeding videos now available online.

42.   It's not necessary to completely launder all your clothing, drapes, sheets, blankets, and other garments to rid them of bed bugs. If these items are already clean, simply run them through the clothes dryer to kill your bed bugs.

43.   Based on their size, bed bugs are capable of hiding nearly anywhere within a home, apartment, or hotel room.

44.   Where do bed bugs come from? The short answer is mommy & daddy bed bugs. However, people get bed bugs from going to places where bed bugs are.

45.   Depending upon your perspective, generally speaking bed bugs are a "people problem." They are not a building problem unless you're the neighbor of someone who brought bed bugs into your building.

46.   Can I get rid of bed bugs myself? It's possible but it takes a lot of work, knowledge, and experience expended over an extended period of time. Most folks are much bet-

ter off leaving bed bug control to a competent pest professional.

47. Are bed bugs resistant to today's chemicals? That's a controversial subject, however bed bugs can be successfully killed by those products that are currently labeled for bed bugs. Within reason, the efficacy of bed bug treatments is more significantly affected by the quality and thoroughness of the bed bug control work performed rather than the products used to kill the bed bugs.

48. Isn't the bed bug problem just a lot of hype being promoted by the media and the pest management industry? Not at all, the incidence of bed bugs is certainly on the rise across the country and, even as an independent pest management consultant that does not advertise, I find that bed bugs take up as much as 50 percent of my time.

49. How can I tell I have bed bugs? Bed bugs are difficult to detect in the early stages. In my opinion, it's rare that a person who unknowingly brings bed bugs home from a trip will discover that she/he did so until they notice that they have been bitten and the problem is already established in their own home.

50. Folks are more likely to notice the telltale signs of bed bugs rather than see the actual live bed bugs themselves.

51. What do bed bug bites look like? People may re-act to bed bug bites differently and the bites may appear differently on different people. Generally speaking, bed bug bites appear as raised reddened bumps on the skin that are usually itchy. There are photos of bed bug bites available for view online.

52. Can I feel the bed bugs bite me? It's doubtful that you will. Bed bugs make their living by being "stealthy." That is, they need to sneak in, find a suitable place to bite, stick in their piercing mouthparts, suck your blood, and sneak away. If you could feel them do this, you'd wake up and simply squish the bed bug. Like mosquitoes, bed bugs inject an anti-coagulant and an anesthetic so you won't feel the bite and the blood flows.

53. Plastic bags and suitable containers can be your best friends in bed bug control and avoidance. Store your clothing and other items that you are 100 percent sure do not have bed bugs in them in a plastic bag and tie it shut to prevent bed bugs from entering. The more things and areas you can make "off limits" to bed bugs, the better for you.

54. Bed bugs can hide in just about anything. In addi-tion to the normal places you'd expect such as beds, mat-tresses, box springs, bed frames, head boards, etc.; we've also found them in places including night stands, clock radios, lamps, shoes, wall hangings, speakers, stereo com-ponents, computers, desks, artificial floral arrangements,

curtains, wall outlets, moldings, door frames, crutches, artificial limbs, pet bedding, toys, plush toys/stuffed animals, clocks, potted plants, furniture, under carpets, fire alarms, telephones, just about everywhere.

55. Just because bed bugs are capable of hiding "just about anywhere" that doesn't mean that they will be "everywhere" within your home. Up until the point that the problem grows to become a "bed bug ground zero" type location it is likely that the bed bugs will be found in areas close to the food in your home which, in reality, is you!

56. Bed bugs will likely hide in areas near where people or their victims sleep. Remember, the victim doesn't have to be a person 100 percent of the time.

57. While bed bugs are commonly active at night, they will feed in the daytime if their host happens to be a night shift worker or a person who maintains such hours. At the end of the day, these are tiny animals and their behavior can vary as individuals or local circumstances dictate.

58. Some people may be bitten over extended periods of time without knowing that they are being bitten. In extreme cases we've seen people experiencing bed bug bites for over a year without them or their medical doctors being able to identify that they in fact have bed bugs.

59. "My husband isn't being bitten and thinks that 'it's all in my head' and that there are no bed bugs. Is this so?" From time to time the lady of the house asks this question and at one home the husband was really dismissive regarding her suspicion of bed bugs in their home. After inspecting his recliner we were able to find six well-fed bed bugs in his La-Z-Boy and advised the woman to ask her husband just whose blood was in them. Your partner may be being bitten but may be one of those people who just doesn't react noticeably nor suffers any itchiness from bed bug bites.

60. "Won't my doctor be able to tell if I have bed bug bites?" Your medical doctors or dermatologist may not know about bed bugs. Medical doctors may have not been trained in medical entomology and, even at best, insect bites can be difficult to detect or diagnose accurately. We once had a woman who was an intensive care nurse who had experienced bed bugs for nearly two years before she discovered that she had a bed bug problem. This woman had been to her general practitioner and was later referred to a dermatologist. She had received prescriptions and treatments for dry skin, psoriasis, seborrhea dermatitis, scabies, and other skin related maladies over the course of those many months when her actual problem was bed bugs.

61. "What's the secret to getting rid of bed bugs?" There is no secret or shortcut to getting rid of bed bugs.

While if caught early on it can be much easier to take care of, the normal experience is that once a person notices that she/he has bed bugs, the problem can be so advanced that a lot of inspection and control work is necessary to rid the property of bed bugs. The real secret is that the control work needs to be very thorough to ensure that no bed bugs escape the control program and the property can be rendered "bed bug free."

62. "I travel for my job. What can I do to prevent picking up bed bugs?" Wow, this is a tough question but you can do what I do. When I check in at a hotel, I enter my room just far enough to be able to close the door behind me. Using my LED flashlight, I then inspect the area around and behind the headboard, the mattress, and the box spring for signs of bed bugs. There are a number of small decent LED flashlights available for about $10 at many retail locations. Luckily thus far, I have yet to encounter bed bugs in any hotel room where I have stayed.

63. "Any other bed bug prevention tips?" Yes, bring large plastic bags with you. I prefer the large white, drawstring plastic trash bags. These bags may be used in two ways; you can put your luggage and other stuff into these bags to prevent bed bugs from entering and, if you think you encountered bed bugs, you can keep the bed bugs trapped within the plastic bags until you have the time to kill them within the bags and keep them from getting into your home. I also know a colleague that places pest strips in his plastic bags as well.

64. "Are there any natural ways to kill bed bugs?" Well, at least to me, it's natural for man to kill bed bugs or any other pest any way possible but that's not what you asked. Suppose you find bed bugs in your shoes or suspect that they are in your luggage. You can places these items in a large black plastic bag and place the bag out in the hot sun for a few hours. If the sun heats the contents of the bag hot enough and long enough, you've killed the bed bugs in a natural way. Note that I said "if." The bed bugs must be heated to a high enough temperature for a long enough period of time to be killed! This means that all the surfaces of the contents must be equally heated throughout and it takes time to get the middle of the teddy bear up to the 113 degrees you're looking for so, take your time and be sure.

65. "If you are going to these bed bug 'ground zero' places all the time, have you ever brought bed bugs home with you?" Well, so far I've been lucky but I do take necessary steps to make sure I don't bring bed bugs home. These steps include; I generally dress in all white and look like an ice cream man when visiting bed bug locations so that I can see bed bugs if they are on me, I'm very careful to not touch or lean on anything in a bed bug location, I keep a Nuvan Pro Strip pest strip within my tool cases just in case, I place my luggage in plastic bags with a pest strip just in case, I keep a change of clothes on hand so that I can change clothes immediately after working at bed bug locations, and when I arrive home I stand in one large plastic bag, then change clothes and put the used clothing into another plastic

bag, and these clothes are then immediately put into the laundry. Shoes, belts, and other non-launderable things are placed in a plastic bag with a pest strip.

66. "How bad can bed bugs get in a home or apartment?" The worst I've seen was an apartment with a sole occupant who was a retired man in his seventies. The apartment was sparsely furnished with just a bed, a table with four chairs, and an upholstered chair in front of a television set on a plastic milk crate. There had to be over ten thousand bed bugs in this apartment. I visited this apartment the day after one of my clients performed a bed bug treatment there for the follow up inspection. Dead bed bugs were mounded like drifted snow in the tracks of the sliding glass door leading to the terrace. Mounds of dead bed bugs were in every corner of every room, along all the floor wall junctions, and the walls were covered with fecal stains. The last surviving few bed bugs were found along the crown moldings. While the application work was very successful, there were still live bed bugs present and follow up treatments were scheduled. Within about 72 hours this person was moved out, the apartment was rendered bed bug free, and totally renovated. Interestingly enough, when I asked this man if he had been bitten by bed bugs he replied that he wasn't and that he had never been bitten in the six months that he had lived in this apartment. It was clear that this person was suffering from mental health-related conditions as well as severe bed bug problems.

67. "What if I only stay at good brand name hotels, will I avoid bed bugs?" As stated previously, bed bugs are a people problem and not a building problem. We've encountered bed bugs in five star locations as well as lower end locations.

68. "How can I avoid moving into an apartment location that has bed bugs?" There are websites that list bed bug problem locations however, after checking on these websites, I have found that they do not verify the information presented, may not update the information on a timely basis and, as such, the information presented may not be reliable. As stated previously, bed bugs are a people problem and not a building problem. If you have concerns ask the lease/rental agent or apartment manager about bed bugs, what they know about them, and what their experience has been regarding bed bugs. A reputable apartment company will be truthful with you and have a sound bed bug management program and policies in place.

69. "How will I know if I'm staying in a bed bug free hotel?" The short answer is you won't. You can ask but my experience is that they will generally give you an answer that indicates that they've never had a bed bug situation. I've asked such questions at locations that I've known have had or are experiencing bed bug situations and this is the sort of reply that I've consistently received. If you do have a concern or suspicion it may be

wise to go ahead and ask your question and be mindful of how your question is answered.

70. "Can I get bed bugs from my neighbor?" Yes, you can. Hungry bed bugs seek out their hosts. They are attracted to heat, carbon dioxide, and other factors given off by their victims. It's possible that bed bugs can find their way from room to room and apartment to apartment through many available pathways.

71. **Remember, a sound bed bug program needs to be thorough! If the program sounds too simple or too good to be true, it probably is.**

72. "Is bed bug work expensive?" Expensive is a relative and subjective term. Bed bug work must be thorough and comprehensive. Currently, there are Pest Management Professional companies doing "state of the art" efficacious bed bug work at fees as high as about $500 per room. At the end of the day, if you have a bed bug problem you want to hire a professional company that does professional work and stands behind their work.

73. **"How do I know if I am hiring a good pest management company to get rid of my bed bugs? "There are thousands of pest management companies in the United States but few who specialize in bed bug control. The bed bug problem is growing in the Unites States and, as a result, the pest management industry is becoming increasingly effective at handling bed bug problems.**

A good bed bug company will have a sound bed bug management program. Their program will be thorough and make sense to you. They will stand behind their work. They will send at least two technicians to do the work. They will provide you with information on how to prepare for the bed bug management work. They will provide you with sound bed bug information. They will answer your questions.

74. "Where can I find reliable information about bed bugs?" There is a lot of good information available online. Generally, I recommend that folks review the information found on unbiased websites including university based websites, medical school websites and others. You can do a search on bed bugs and find many references to learn more about bed bugs. The more you know, the better equipped you are to make good decisions.

75. "I'm a homeowner, should I spray the home myself to prevent bed bugs?" The decision to apply pesticide products in your own home is solely up to you and, generally speaking, homeowners are free from the regulations that Pest Management Professionals must comply with when applying pesticides. However, for the most part, while we all wish to maintain a pest-free environment, we also wish to limit or avoid any unnecessary exposure to pesticides within our homes and the environment if possible. Let's be very careful when considering pesticide use and application and take care to implement some of the non-chemical dependent pre-

ventative measures to avoid pest problems in the first place. Being careful and using the preventative techniques mentioned elsewhere in this article is likely a wiser way to go than spraying pesticides unnecessarily.

76. "What sort of places have you seen bed bug problems occur?" Wow, the list of places that the pest management industry has been called in to handle bed bug problems is long and disconcerting. Bed bugs can be anywhere that man is and they have been, so let's leave it at that as we don't wish to unnecessarily alarm anyone.

77. **If necessary, bed bugs can feed on your pets so don't forget your pet's bedding if you need to do bed bug work in your home.**

78. Generally, folks who unknowingly bring bed bugs home do not discover that they have a problem for anywhere from weeks to months.

79. **Based upon my experience, most homeowner folks who have a bed bug problem have one thing in common; they have traveled and brought bed bugs home with them from a business trip or vacation.**

80. "My house has been treated for bed bugs, what should I do now?" Be careful to utilize all the preventative techniques and follow the directions provided to you by your Pest Management Professional.

81. "My apartment company has a pest control provider, should I hire my own to take care of my apartment?" Generally speaking, you are able to hire a pest professional to take care of pest situations within your own apartment at your own expense and, because you hired them yourself, they work directly for you and may provide you with superior service. However, contact your landlord company and ask questions about the bed bug services being provided by their pest professional before you make a decision as to what's best for you.

82. "The neighboring apartment has a bed bug problem, what should I do?" If you suspect that the neighboring apartment has a bed bug problem this does not necessarily mean that your apartment will get bed bugs. However, it is possible for bed bugs to travel from apartment to apartment by various means so you are wise to be concerned. Contact the apartment company/landlord to express your concerns, find out what they are doing about the bed bug situation, find out what they are doing to assure that they prevent a problem from getting into your apartment, and maintain a level of increased vigilance opposite bed bugs. If after doing this you have continued questions and concerns, be persistent and make decisions in your best interest to avoid bed bugs.

83. "In hotels, why is the headboard area a prime spot to find bed bugs?" Bed bugs prefer to hide in undisturbed areas. In a hotel, the maid changes the sheets daily or at least regularly. As such, the mattress becomes

less of a desirable hiding place for bed bugs. The headboard is close by and seldom moved or disturbed. However, with bed bugs, we are dealing with live animals and once again, your mileage may vary.

84. "Do bed bug traps work?" There are new bed bug traps being introduced to the Pest Management Professional market and my suspicion is that such traps will soon be marketed to the general public. Those traps that emit certain bed bug attractants including heat, carbon dioxide, octanol, and other materials have demonstrated high attractiveness to bed bugs. Simple trap designs, such as the Climb-Up Interceptor unit by McNight, that rely on the bed bugs' inability to climb smooth surfaces have also demonstrated effectiveness and are economical.

85. "Can't I simply wrap my mattress and box spring in plastic rather than by an expensive mattress encasement?" Yes you can, but if you have ever slept on plastic you probably found it very uncomfortable. In the field I have seen folks take desperate measures to combat their bed bug problems. I've seen them wrap their beds in plastic and shower curtains but these plastic covers usually rip and we need to make sure that we have 100 percent coverage. The Mattress Safe and Protect-A-Bed covers are well built, tested bed bug proof, dependable, comfortable to sleep on, and widely available.

86. Heat can be used successfully to kill bed bugs in items that cannot be laundered or treated with conventional pesticides.

87. Pest strips containing DDVP are now labeled for bed bugs. DDVP provides 100 percent control of bed bugs.

88. All products currently labeled for bed bugs will kill bed bugs on contact at labeled rates. Residual efficacy of such products against bed bugs varies and is dependent upon a variety of conditions.

89. Bed bug-sniffing dogs are effective at finding bed bugs. After learning about such dogs, my opinion is that those dogs that are trained and used only for bed bug work are superior to multi-pest detection dogs. And, dogs should be NESDCA certified. Check out nesdca.com for more information.

90. "I'm a pest professional that does a lot of bed bug work, should I purchase my own dog?" While that decision is totally up to you, understand that such a dog is a significant commitment. These dogs are not pets! They are additional trained employees of your company. The dog's training must be maintained and an effective dog requires a dedicated and well trained handler. Speak with a bed bug dog trainer, learn as much as you can, and then make your decision. The initial cost for a bed bug-trained dog

can be about $10,000 however, the cost to maintain the dog, the handler, and keep up with the long term training must also be considered.

91. Bed bug detection dog services may be hired to help you with certain bed bug situations and you'll likely find this more cost effective for you.

92. People who travel regularly are more susceptible and likely to bring home bed bugs than people who don't. As an example, when conducting German cockroach field trials in section eight housing recently, we had hundreds of apartments that were virtually loaded with German cockroaches and not one with bed bugs. Within five miles of this location we worked at an apartment complex of nearly four hundred apartments whose residents were of international origin and nearly every cockroach-infested apartment also had bed bugs.

93. Bed bug fecal stains on walls will run when sprayed with water.

94. Bed bugs crawl at about the same speed as argentine ants or odorous house ants.

95. Generally speaking, more bed bugs are found toward the head of the bed than toward the foot of the bed.

96. There are many bed bug videos that can be seen online if you do a proper search.

97. **Two years ago Bayer environmental Science produced an excellent bed bug training video on DVD featuring Dr. Austin M. Frishman and Joe Barile. Check with your local distributor or Bayer representative to get a copy of this video.**

98. There are many folks working behind the scenes in the pest management industry on new bed bug products and techniques, stay tuned.

99. **Used properly, steam will kill 100 percent of the bed bugs and bed bug eggs on contacted.**

100. Continuous fill professional steamers will allow you to work longer and more efficiently than non-reservoir continuous fill steam units.

101. **Homeowner type steamers normally used for wall paper removal are not good choices forbed bug control.**

102. Bed bug eggs are glued in place and bed bugs can hold on surprisingly well against a vacuum. However, it is beneficial to use a vacuum to remove as many bed bugs as possible as part of your bed bug management program.

103. "Hey, that's a lot of bed bug information. It seems like you know all there is to know about bed bugs?" Whoa, hold on there. Field experience has taught me that none of us know "all there is to know" about most things, especially bed bugs. Each day presents additional opportunities for all of us to learn more about bed bugs, and new stuff is being discovered and developed every day.

104. Be on a constant search to increase your knowledge of bed bugs and the successful management of bed bugs. The pest management industry provides an important service to the public. No one deserves to suffer the inconvenience, agony, and deleterious effects of life with bed bugs!

Paul J. Bello, President
PJB Pest Management
Consulting, LLC

FINAL THOUGHTS

There is no final thought, just a continual one. We are just beginning to tackle this rising bed bug problem. How we meet the challenge sets the tone for future challenges. Should we go backward and use larger amounts of insecticides? Will we wait until industries decide it is profitable before investing in new technologies that will solve the problem? Will the government decide it is better to fine landlords and therefore raise revenue rather than to assist in helping the handicapped, elderly, and our children? Will we have to deal with the demons of the night in every other home before we eradicate them again? At this time there are more questions than answers.

I will leave each of you with this encouragement—you can fix this problem. Think and write your local legislator. Get involved. Be vigilant and caring of your neighbors. I only ask you to try your best. This will take time and effort on all our parts. We will get through it and this time the knowledge will not be lost. It must not be lost. For the sake of the next generation.

APPENDIX A

How to Choose a Pest Control Company

1. Is the company registered to apply pesticide in the state? Check with the state's agency or consumer affairs for this information.
2. How long has the company been in business?
3. Do they have any complaints or members with the Better Business Bureau, Chamber of Commerce, or Consumer Affairs? If so, how many and did they resolve the issues?
4. Is the company a member of the National Pest Management Association or State Association?

5. Are the technicians working for the company certified? This implies that the technicians have taken pest control courses and exams.

6. Does the company provide continuing education courses for their technicians? This way you know that the technicians are receiving the latest methods in treatment and technology.

7. Do they have an entomologist on staff or on retainer? This helps in resolving the tough pest issues.

8. What is their customer service department like? Ask friends or neighbor who use the company.

9. Ask the company for referrals. Ask the clients if all their needs were met and what the process was like.

10. Is the initial inspector or agent neat, clean, and professional? Did they arrive on time? Is he knowledgeable? Will he customize the pest program to fit your needs and budget?

11. Compare prices with two or more companies.

12. Don't just choose the lowest price or the highest price. This is not always the best indicator of the service you will receive.

13. Make sure that you and the pest control company are clear with the terms of the contract, the length, and the services. Don't just settle on the price.

14. Ask for a certificate of insurance. This should cover both property damage and personal injury.

15. Will you have a charge for every visit or are no-charge services provided for unscheduled services?

16. Does the company provide exclusion services, or do you need to hire a contractor?

17. Will the company provide the labels to the products that they intend to use prior to service?
18. Does the company provide a preparation sheet with information on how to prepare your home for treatment?
19. Will they assist in the preparation, such as bagging, laundering, storage, or do they recommend a subcontractor?
20. Do they provide other services, such as thermal remediation treatment in the home?
21. Do they have a heat chamber?
22. If they provide "Green Pest Control Service," what makes the service green? Who certified them as green— is it an independent agency?
23. What is the cancellation policy of the contract?
24. Don't get pressured into anything, and remember they work for you. Customer service is as important as the treatment. Remember you are going through enough with the bed bugs.
25. Don't make a hasty decision when choosing a company. Wait a few hours or until the next day if possible to make sure you've done your research.

APPENDIX B

The National Pest Management Association is now in the process of creating a best practices guide. As the following reprinted article states:

NPMA ESTABLISHES BLUE RIBBON
BED BUG TASK FORCE

November 16, 2010 (Fairfax, Va.) The National Pest Management Association (NPMA) is pleased to announce the establishment of the NPMA Blue Ribbon Bed Bug Task Force, a broad-based stakeholder group whose goal is the development of an industry-wide comprehensive response to the bed bug pandemic sweeping the globe, including education, best practices, policy, and research.

"The Bed Bug Blue Ribbon Task Force is simultaneously addressing a broad range of topics," stated NPMA Senior Vice President Bob Rosenberg, "but will focus initially on the development of best practices for bed bug inspections and treatment, including K-9 inspections. The task force's efforts are designed to ensure that the pest management industry remains at the forefront of the war on bed bugs and ensure the continued credibility of the industry with consumers, media and policy makers."

During an organizational meeting at PestWorld, NPMA's recent annual conference and exposition, the task force identified four key areas on which it will focus. These key areas are Best Management Practices, Credentialing, Certification, and Training; Public Policy; Public Outreach, Education, Messaging and Data Needs; and Research and Efficacy.

Workgroups were assigned to each of these key areas. The following individuals have been appointed to each workgroup:

Best Practices

Lonnie Alonso, Columbus Pest Control, OH
Chris Arne, Rentokil - Ehrlich/Presto-X, PA

Matt Beal, OH Department of Agriculture
Judy Black, The Steritech Group, NC
Michael Botha, Sandwich Isle Pest Solutions, HI
Jay Bruesch, Plunkett's Pest Control, Inc., MN
Norman Goldenberg, Terminix International, TN
Ron Harrison, Orkin Pest Control, GA
Debra Kay, Envirotech Pest Solutions, CO
Stephen Kells, University of Minnesota
Todd Leyse, Adams Pest Control, Inc., MN
Dini Miller, Virginia Tech University
Matt Nixon, American Pest Management, MD
Mark Sheperdigian, Rose Pest Solutions, MI
Scott Steckel, Varment Guard environmental Services, Inc., OH
Rich Stevenson, Modern Pest Services, ME
Alfie Treleven, Sprague Pest Solutions, WA
Louis Witherington, Falcon Termite & Pest, FL

Public Policy

Matt Beal, OH Department of Agriculture
Donnie Blake, Okolona Pest Control, Inc., KY
Norman Goldenberg, Terminix International, TN
Susan Jones, Ohio State University
Mike Katz, Western Exterminator, CA
Mark Sheperdigian, Rose Pest Solutions, MI
Rich Stevenson, Modern Pest Services, ME

Public Outreach

Dave Burns, Burns Pest Solutions, AZ

Liza Fleeson, VA Department of Agriculture & Consumer Services

Gail Getty, University of California

Andrew Klein, Assured Environments, NY

Mark O'Hara, Anderson Pest Solutions, IL

Phil Cooper, Cooper Pest Solutions, NJ

Mike Rottler, Rottler Pest & Lawn Solutions, MO

Alfie Treleven, Sprague Pest Solutions, WA

Research & Efficacy

Michael Botha, Sandwich Isle Pest Solutions, HI

Jay Bruesch, Plunkett's Pest Control, Inc., MN

Steve Dwinell, FL Department of Agriculture and Consumer Services

Ron Harrison, Orkin Pest Control, GA

Susan Jones, Ohio State University

Stephen Kells, University of Minnesota

Phil Koehler, University of Florida

Dini Miller, Virginia Tech University

Lois Rossi, U.S. environmental Protection Agency

Changlu Wang, Rutgers University

Each workgroup is scheduled to meet within the next two weeks to identify scope and timeline, with initial deliverables scheduled to be available at the National Bed Bug Forum, January 5-7 in Denver, Colorado. Information about the task force and all task force documents are available at www.npmapestworld.org/publicpolicy/ task_ force.cfm.

The NPMA, a non-profit organization with more than 7,000 members, was established in 1933 to support the pest management industry's commitment to the protection of public health, food and property.

REFERENCES

Elliot, L. *Medieval Medicine and the Plague*. Canada: Crabtree Publishing Company, 2006.

Johnson, C. G. "Development, hatching, and mortality of the eggs of *Cimex lectularius* (hemiptera) in relation to climate, with observations on the effects of preconditioning to temperature." *Parasitology* 32 (1940): 127–173.

———. "The longevity of fasting bed bug (*C. lectularius*) under experimental conditions and particularly in relation to the saturation deficiency law of water loss." *Parasitology* 32 (1940a): 239–270.

Mallis, Arnold. *Handbook of Pest Control, 8th ed*. Mallis Handbook & Technical Training Company, 1997.

Mallis, Arnold. *Handbook of Pest Control, 4th ed*. Mallis Handbook & Technical Training Company, 1964.

Potter, M.F. "The history of bed bug management: lessons from the past." *Pest Control Technology* 36(8) (2008): 12.

Schuh, R.T. and J.A. Slater. *True Bugs of the World (Hemiptera Heteroptera)*. Ithaca: Cornell University Press, 1995.

USDA. "Bed Bugs: How to Control Them." Leaflet 337, 1953.

Usinger, R.L. *Monograph of Cimicidae (Hemiptera Heteroptera)*. Maryland: Entomological Society of America, 1966.

Vlasov, Y.A. *Russian Journal of Tropical Medicine* 7 (1929): 688–692.

www.askthebugman.com Comprehensive animal welfare site managed by Robert Fagerlund

www.magicexterminating.com This is the company I work for. They cover the five boroughs of New York City and Western Nassau County in New York State.

www.suburbanexterminating.com This is Magic's sister company and they cover Eastern Nassau County and all of Suffolk County in New York State.

www.class-insecta.com My personal web site with information on many different insects.

www.bedbugregistry.com Over 20,000 reports in 12,000 locations in the United States and Canada of bed bug activity. It lists locations of hotels and apartment buildings with reported infestations.

www.newyorkvsbedbugs.org This site is managed by Renee Corea. A tremendous resource on bed bugs.

www.usda.gov Search "bed bugs" on this site and you will get official government resources on bed bugs.

www.epa.gov Another government website with bed bug resources.

www.pestcontrolcanada.com A Canadian-based pest control resource for all provinces

www.chroniclingamerica.loc.gov The library of congress web site which has digital copies of old newspapers from around the country on any topic. Search for "bed bugs."

http://medent.usyd.edu.au/bedbug A resource to Code of Practice from Australia by Stephen L. Doggett PhD.

www.nysipm.cornell.edu/publications/bb_guidelines The New York State IPM guideline bulletin.

www.nyc.gov/html/doh/downloads/pdf/vector/bedbug-guide.pdf New York City's bed bug advisory board's bed bug guide.

www.greenshieldcertified.org The independent certification organization that certifies companies as green.

www.pestworld.org The National Pest Management Association. They will help in finding a local certified and insured pest management company in your state.

www.pctonline.com One of the pest management trade magazines.

www.mypmp.net One of the pest management trade magazines.

Search your own state cooperative extension program for bulletins related to your state.